Presented to :

_____

From :

_____

Date :

_____

BY Mildred Tengbom

A Life to Cherish
Especially for Mother

Especially For Mother

Mildred Tengbom

Fleming H. Revell Company
Old Tappan, New Jersey

"Homage to Ma Miller" by Wilton Sankawula from *Resource* magazine, December, 1966. Copyright *Learning With* magazine. Used by permission.

"When the Baby Came" by Barbara A. Jones. Copyright 1976 by Christian Herald Ass'n.

"Tell Me" by Isobel Mortimer from DECISION © 1969 by the Billy Graham Evangelistic Association.

"The Business" by Ida Barton from DECISION © 1971 by the Billy Graham Evangelistic Association.

"Lord Jesus Fill the Gap" from *The Gift of Inner Healing* by Ruth Stapleton Carter © 1976. Used by permission of Word Books, Publishers, Waco, Tx.

Quotations by Dorothy Sayers are from *Are Women Human?* © 1971. Used by permission of Wm. B. Eerdmans Publishing Co.

Quotations by V. M. Stewart are from The Movement of the Spirit Challenges a Feminist: A Reaction. *Journal of Psychology and Theology,* 1974, 2(4), 311–317.

"A Parent's Prayer" by Dr. Garry C. Myers used by permission of HIGHLIGHTS FOR CHILDREN, INC., Columbus, Ohio.

"The Heart of the Childless Is Gladdened With Children" is based on "When the Answer Is No" from IS YOUR GOD BIG ENOUGH? by Mildred Tengbom, copyright 1973 Augsburg Publishing House. Used by permission.

"How to Develop Good Relationships With Adolescent Children" from THE BONUS YEARS by Mildred Tengbom, copyright 1975, Augsburg Publishing House. Used by permission.

"The Faith of a Mother—Monica, Mother of Augustine" from THE CONFESSIONS OF AUGUSTINE IN MODERN ENGLISH by Sherwood Eliot Wirt. Copyright © 1971 by Sherwood Eliot Wirt under the title, LOVE SONG. Reprinted by Zondervan Publishing House under the above title, 1977. Used by permission.

"The Baby" from PRAYERS by Michel Quoist, Copyright, 1963, Sheed and Ward, New York.

Library of Congress Cataloging in Publication Data

Main entry under title:

Especially for mother.

1. Mothers—Prayer-books and devotions—
English. I. Tengbom, Mildred.
BV4847.E86   242'.6'43   77-16027
ISBN 0-8007-0911-X
ISBN 0-8007-0915-2 gift ed.

TO my own mother
  and others who have mothered me
  and to the five who have made motherhood such a joy for
    me:
TO my husband, Luverne,
  to Dan, Judy, Janet, and David
  this book is gratefully dedicated

Contents

The Book Our Mother Read

We search the world for truth; we cull
The good, the pure, the beautiful,
From graven stone and written scroll,
And all old flower-fields of the soul;
And, weary seekers of the best,
We come back laden from the quest,
To find that all the sages said
Is in the Book our mothers read.

JOHN GREENLEAF WHITTIER

*Especially
For Mother*

Motherhood
as Missionary Support

Bear one another's burdens, and so fulfil the law of Christ.

Galatians 6:2 RSV

The week at a conference had been so wonderful in every way. I caught myself sighing a little as I thought of returning to the daily care schedule of a home. Before I had left, I had received a card from a friend. On the outside a little girl sat on top of a cloud. Inside, the card said simply, "That's all right. You can come down when you get home." I didn't know if I wanted to come down. Dirty laundry and dishes have a way of deflating me. I sighed again.

Then I chided myself. After all, I was coming home to a loving family. And Janet would have everything in order. For a sixteen-year-old, I admitted to myself, she took care of a house unusually well.

Our 747 broke through the low-lying mustard smog pall of Los Angeles. Minutes later our wheels touched ground. We rolled to a stop. I had come home.

I came home to a husband standing as near to the ramp door as he could. I blew a kiss; he beamed and waved.

Home to fourteen-year-old David, who had spurted past me in height while I had been gone.

"Your hair needs to be shampooed," I observed.

"Can't," he said, holding aloft a right forefinger encased in a splint.

"Broken?"

David nodded.

"How? Football?"

He grinned. "I wore my tan cords the whole time you were gone, too," he said and grinned again.

"What's wrong with Janet?" I asked a bit irritably. "Couldn't she have shampooed your hair? Didn't she wash clothes?"

"Janet's busy," David said briefly, and then he was out the door, answering a friend's call to come and referee.

I came home to one dead plant and two languishing ones, to a kitchen counter top that needed to be scoured, to sticky handles of cupboard doors, to a fridge needing to be wiped out, half a cup of sugar in the sugar canister, a freezer stripped of almost all the goodies I had prepared before leaving, an overflowing laundry basket.

In the living room I found a beautiful potted chrysanthemum plant. A sheet of paper under it had welcome-home and love messages from our four teenagers. I studied it. "Were Dan and Judy home?"

"Mm huh." My husband was reading his mail. "With their roommates. Dan brought his laundry."

"What did you give them to eat?"

"TV dinners."

"And left-overs." Dave had popped in the house again. "Janet dug everything she could out of the fridge. Sure goin' to be nice to have a decent meal again."

"Did you suffer?"

Young boy woes poured out. "And you should've seen the house before yesterday. Dad was running the vacuum cleaner and was down on his hands and knees scrubbin' the kitchen floor." Chuckles followed. "It had gotten so sticky we almost lost our boots every time we took a step."

"I'll bet." I turned to Luverne. "But how come? Janet did better than that two years ago when I left. She was only fourteen then."

Luverne hesitated. "Janet isn't thinking too much about food or laundry these days," he said slowly and then added, "but don't scold her."

Janet didn't get home until quarter to five. I had been waiting for her since quarter after three. It was, after all, the afternoon I had come home.

I heard the screen door open and shut. Janet dumped her books on the counter and sank into a chair.

"Hi, Mom! How'd your meetings go?"

"*Fan*-tastic! Better 'n anything I had ever dreamed."

"Oh, yeah. That's great. But then, the Lord's promised to do more than we expect . . . . Anything cool in the fridge to drink?"

"You're late. Where've you been?" I bit my tongue, but the words already were out.

"School."

"All this time?"

She spread-eagled her arms on the counter and rested her head on her arms. "There's this girl who keeps talking about suicide. I took my Bible and talked with her about Jesus . . . . It's going to be nice to have breakfast tomorrow."

"Breakfast? Haven't you eaten? You've been getting up at 6:30 and not eating?"

"I haven't been getting up at 6:30. Been so tired. Jean's been coming over at night to get help with biology . . . . She's really got it rough, you know. Her mom and dad drink and fight. They couldn't care less what happens to Jeannie. She was getting *D*'s. Now she's getting *B*'s. She's real happy about that."

I got up and began to survey the contents of the fridge and pantry.

"I've been thinking," I said, "I guess I won't die yet for a while."

"Whaddya say?!"

"I said I don't think I'll die yet for a while. I think I'm needed around here."

Her face lit up with a happy grin. "You better believe it!"

I smiled too. The realization that caring for my family not only met their needs but set them free to love and help others put a rainbow around my domestic chores. With a singing heart I slipped on an apron and began to make dinner.

On Work

All work is empty save when there is love . . . .
And what is it to work with love?
It is to weave the cloth with threads drawn from your heart,
    even as if your beloved were to wear that cloth.
It is to build a house with affection, even as if your beloved
    were to dwell in that house.
It is to sow seeds with tenderness and reap the harvest with joy,
    even as if your beloved were to eat the fruit.
It is to charge all things you fashion with a breath of your own
    spirit . . . .
Work is love made visible.
And if you cannot work with love but only with distaste, it is
    better that you should leave your work and sit at the gate of
    the temple and take alms of those who work with joy.
For if you bake bread with indifference, you bake a bitter bread
    that feeds but half man's hunger.
And if you grudge the crushing of the grapes, your grudge
    distils a poison in the wine.
And if you sing though as angels, and love not the singing, you
    muffle man's ears to the voices of the day and the voices of
    the night.

KAHLIL GIBRAN

Directions

Do not have your concert first and tune your instruments afterward. Begin the day with God.

HUDSON TAYLOR

Some days I feel like a centipede,
only different,
for my hundred legs
do not propel me steadily forward
in only one direction,
but all hundred legs
seem to be scurrying in a hundred different directions,
and *ouch!*
I'm pulled apart at the core.
Wife, mother,
housekeeper, writer, author, teacher, lecturer,
friend, comforter, disciplinarian,
student, consumer, bookkeeper,
cook, baker, gardener,
chauffeur, messenger, courier,
hostess, appointment maker,
guardian of the family's physical, spiritual, and emotional
    health,
citizen, public servant, church person,
supporter of Worthy Causes—
on and on the list goes.
The longer I live
the wider and wider my circle ripples out,
until I become frightened

and anxious that I shall become so splintered and fragmented
that no wholeness will remain.
Is distraction the inevitable lot of mothers?
Is there no way out?
What causes the fragmentation?
Are ever-widening interests bane or blessing?
I struggle with these questions.

In choosing to be a wife and mother, I tell myself,
I committed myself to some of these distractions.
They are my calling.
They are life.

At the same time, should not I ask myself some questions?
Have I assumed responsibilities that other members of my fam-
    ily could profitably carry?
Have I let others determine how clean my oven shall be, how
    involved my children shall become in school and church
    activities, how many organizations I shall be active in, how
    often I remodel my home?
Or have I taken time to be alone and quiet and probe deep into
    my heart and discover what means most of all to me?
And having made that discovery, have I dared to be true to it?
WOMEN: STILL SECOND BUT TRYING HARDER, the news article
    headlines.
Is this the root of some of my feverish activity?
Trying harder to be what:
successful, famous, socially accepted, loved, acknowledged,
    well paid, provider of privileges and luxuries for our chil-
    dren?
Or trying harder to be a whole person?
Would that it were so!
At the end of life,
when I look back over my years,
what will make me feel best
about the way I've spent those years?
Will pondering this help to unify my life?

But even in this I need guidance and direction
from the Transcendent One,

from God, who knows best.
For, left to my own rationalization,
I could easily be led astray.
Was this not why Jesus,
speaking to the harried activists of His day,
uttered words applicable to me too:
"Seek *first* the kingdom of God and His righteousness."

This goal, then, becomes for me the solid, central core
from which all activities can branch out
so that my hundred feet,
instead of scurrying aimlessly in all directions,
as sheep frightened and scattered by a strange, barking dog,
will move me steadily forward and upward
like the many steps of a moving escalator,
encased within a well-defined path
that leads unerringly to the destination
at the top.

Tell Me

What a mess everything is—
nine o'clock
not a single child asleep
evening wasted and nothing's done.
I feel exhausted
overcome
wishing there was hope in sight,
light at the end of the tunnel.
If only I had someone to chat with,
someone who would understand
how I feel—
Oh, God, however can I get through
all this?

God?
Of course!

Nearer than breathing—
closer than hands and feet—
how could I have taken so long to think of You?
Forgive me, Lord.
Tell it to me again.
You are the Overcomer;
in Your presence is fulness of joy,
and strength enough for all
I have to do
tonight.

ISOBEL MORTIMER

If women *liked* everlasting work they would not be human beings at all. *Being* human beings, they like work just as much and just as little as anybody else. They dislike perpetual washing and cooking just as much as perpetual typing and standing behind shop counters. Some of them prefer typing to scrubbing—but that does not mean that they are not, as human beings, entitled to blast the typewriter when they feel that way. There is perhaps only one human being in a thousand who is passionately interested in his job for his job's sake.

DOROTHY SAYERS

My Doctor's Paraphrase of the Twenty-third Psalm

The Lord is my pacemaker,
  I shall not rush.
He makes me stop and rest at quiet intervals.
He provides me with images of stillness which restore my serenity.
He leads me in ways of efficiency through calmness of mind,
  and His guidance is sure.
Even though I have a great many things to accomplish each day,

I will not fret,
for His presence is here.

His timelessness and all-importance
will keep me in balance.
By anointing my mind with His oil of tranquility
my cup of joyous energy overflows.
Surely harmony and effectiveness
shall be the fruit of my hours,
for I shall walk at the pace of my Lord,
and dwell in His house forever.

AUTHOR UNKNOWN

The habit of thinking about work as something one does to
make money is so ingrained in us that we can scarcely imagine
what a revolutionary change it would be to think about it instead in terms of the work done.

DOROTHY SAYERS

Peter's Five Guidelines

The great commitment is so much easier than the ordinary everyday one—and can all too easily shut our hearts to the latter.

DAG HAMMARSKJÖLD

The children are in school and I have some free time.
How shall I spend it?
I don't really want to box myself into a nine-to-five schedule.
My husband and I would rather do with a little less than have
     both of us committed to fifty-week yearly schedules.
But the free hours are there for me to invest.
How shall I spend them wisely?

"How do you know how best to invest your life?" I asked some
     of my friends at a dinner table one night.
"I have some guidelines I follow," said Peter Wagner, professor
     at Fuller Theological Seminary. "Perhaps they will be of
     help to you too. Five points there are," he said, his fingers
     outlining the five arms of the candelabrum on the table
     before us.

"Point number one.
As objectively as you can, try to understand what spiritual gifts
     God has given you. Start by studying Romans 12, 1 Corin-
     thians 12, and Ephesians 4."
I nodded.

"Point number two.
Venture out and try to use these gifts."
"That makes sense," I said.

"Point number three is: Evaluate what degree of success follows
    as you use your gifts."
"Interesting—but valid," I commented.

"Point number four.
Examine your own inner feelings and responses as you develop
    your abilities and put them to work."
"Hmm," I said. "That's one I never thought of before. But it
    surely would make a difference with some of the things I've
    become involved in but don't enjoy."

"And point number five," our friend concluded, "is to seek
    additional confirmation from a few Christian friends who
    know you well but will be honest with you."
I nodded again, thinking of times my friends, often unsolicited,
    had offered advice and observations that had helped me
    see and understand my strengths and weaknesses and
    called me forth to new ventures of faith.

Five guidelines of Peter Wagner's
to help us understand
how best to invest our most precious treasures:
our lives and our time.
These guidelines have helped me.
Perhaps they'll offer direction to you too.

Lord, Give Me Wisdom and Discipline

Lord, give me the wisdom and discipline
    to plan my days and weeks
    to allow for free time:
uncluttered time to dream, think, meditate, and plan—
    to struggle with understanding the lessons
    You are wanting to teach me through life,
    so these experiences will not be wasted.
I need time to think about present-day trends,
    and how these affect

our nation,
  community,
  and our family—
time to search for answers to problems
  instead of continuing to buck my head against them.
I long for time to read,
  to listen,
  to develop ideas,
  to take advantage of surprise opportunities.
Let me find time occasionally to revel in the beauty of Your
    sunsets and sunrises,
  to watch clouds float by overhead,
  to listen to crickets chirp and frogs croak,
  to play Monopoly with our children in front of the fire,
  to bake bread,
  to sniff the freshness of the earth after rain,
  to feel the coolness of moist sand between my toes,
  to soak in the expansiveness and wonder of Your creation
    long enough to burst into spontaneous praise,
  to feel the rapid heartbeat of a child who clings close to me,
  to give my gift of a relaxed, pleasant evening to my friends as
    I entertain them,
  to be awed by the insights I receive as I study Your Word,
  to know Your inexpressible peace seeping into my heart as I
    unhurriedly commune in prayer with You,
    and learn to really worship You.

Lord, the time is mine,
  a gift from You.
But give me, oh, give me, the Mary-heart
  that will treasure
  time
  for building soul strengths and inner resources.
Lord, give me wisdom and discipline.

Heavenly Father,
whose life is within us and
whose love is ever about us,
grant that your life may be maintained in our lives today and
    every day
as with gladness of heart,
  without haste
  or confusion of thought,
we go about our daily tasks,
  conscious of ability to meet every rightful demand,
  seeing the larger meaning of little things,
  and finding beauty and love everywhere.
And in the sense of your presence
may we walk through the hours,
  breathing the atmosphere of love,
  rather than anxious striving.

AUTHOR UNKNOWN

I Learned From the Trees

All living relationships are in process of change, of expansion, and must perpetually be building themselves new forms.

ANNE MORROW LINDBERGH

Our family was resting in Yellowstone Park, homeward bound for California after a 3,000 mile vacation trip. With six persons cooped up in the car for so many days, little habits and idiosyncrasies began to irritate each of us. These shortcomings loomed so large that I was quite convinced that as a Christian and a mother I was a failure.

Dejected, I left the family and walked across the campgrounds to the amphitheater overlooking Yellowstone Lake. It lay calm, blue green, shimmering and sparkling with the rays of the setting sun. On the opposite side of the lake, far in the distance the Teton Mountains were boldly etched against the sky.

But it was the trees around the amphitheater that caught my attention: slender lodgepole pine, bushy spruce, and sweeping firs, rustling poplars. I let my eyes dwell on their beauty.

Then I began to study each tree in detail. Not one was perfectly straight. Two whose tops had been heavily laden with snow were arched like a bow. One tall beauty was marred because its top was only a skeleton of naked, twisted branches. A few had split trunks. One was knobby with warts.

Suddenly I realized that nature's norm is not perfection. Yet, despite the imperfections, viewed as a whole, the forest was wondrously beautiful. Startled, I realized that for the children of God, perfection is not the norm either. In my pursuit of the highest for myself and my family, I had become absorbed with

26

faults so that I could not be cheered and uplifted by the worthy aspects.

Now, as I headed back to my family, I prayed God would more often help me see the beauty of my young forest.

When you love someone, you do not love them all the time, in exactly the same way, from moment to moment. It is an impossibility. It is even a lie to pretend to. And yet this is exactly what most of us demand. We have so little faith in the ebb and flow of life, of love, of relationships. We leap at the flow of the tide and resist in terror its ebb . . . . Security in a relationship lies in living in the present relationship and accepting it as it is now.

ANNE MORROW LINDBERGH

The worst impediment to a satisfying family life today is the conviction that it should be free of serious difficulties, and should run like a smoothly working machine. If the correct view prevailed—that when people live together this, in itself, creates problems—then it could be seen that the good family isn't one in which problems don't occur, but one in which the members work together to solve problems as they happen.

DR. BRUNO BETTELHEIM

It is unrealistic to expect any relationship to be all-giving and all-nurturing.

CLINEBELL AND CLINEBELL

My Children Have Become Strangers

Rare moments of sharing with adolescent children can also help the parent to reopen and re-live some of his own youth by sharing in his children's growth.

CLINEBELL AND CLINEBELL

My children have become strangers in their own home.
I sense this change when they return
   from college
   for brief holidays.
The first two or three days exuberance, joy, gaiety over-
    flow:
   impulsive hugs,
   outbursts of song,
   from the girls giggles and laughter.
But as the days pass a subtle change takes place,
faintly disguised annoyance over the restrictions and schedules
    family living asks of everyone in a home,
retreats to the bedroom,
the I-don't-want-to-talk-to-anyone message coming through
    the closed door,
pensive moods, discontent, restlessness, inquietude.
But squeals of joy when a friend from school calls.
Animated conversation about what it will be like to be back
    among their friends.
I watch, observe, listen to it all,
   recall my own youth,
   and understand:
home, yet homeless.
I know the thoughts that chase up and down the corridors of
    their minds:
   "I don't really belong at home anymore.

But where do I belong?
I feel at home with my friends at school,
but at the same time—sadness covers me as I think of it—
I know that on graduation day
we shall part,
many of us never to meet again.
Then where will *home* be?''

Ah, my children, you are perplexed and searching,
 not quite understanding
 that for most of you,
 meeting and committing yourself to the one who will be your
  lifelong partner
 will be coming home,
 will *really* be coming home.

For those of you for whom life's walk will be in single solitari-
  ness coming home will be more difficult.
For hard-to-describe, restless, searching longings will always
  play about within your heart.
Those longings you will have to learn
 to live with and assuage as best you can
 by loving your God
 and reaching out in unselfish love to others.
It may help you, too, to understand
 that even your brothers and sisters
 who "come home" when they meet their mates,
 occasionally still feel homeless.
In one sense
 we all are,
 for none of us will ever fully be "at home"
 until we are at home with God.

And how do I, as a mother, feel,
 as I silently, and sometimes with an aching heart,
 watch these struggles of our children?
Feelings interchange—
 satisfaction that they are maturing,
 questioning myself: Have I adequately prepared them for
  this?

wistful longing that I could make life's adjustments easier for
   them,
assurance that God will see them through
   and make them stronger and more authentic,
because we allow them
   the freedom
   to feel homeless at home.
We accept their feelings
   and do not chide, misunderstand,
   or try to fill an aching void we never can fill.

Our children have become strangers in our home,
   for a new adventure
   is beckoning them,
   but I know that
   when they have pursued their quest to its end,
   they will again
   be "at home" while at home with us,
   although in a different way.
Contented then,
   thankful
   and appreciative
   to be
   back at home.

The Crown of the Home is Godliness;
The Beauty of the Home is Order;
The Glory of the Home is Hospitality;
The Blessing of the Home is Contentment.

HENRY VAN DYKE

"What," men have asked distractedly from the beginning of
time, "what on earth do women want?" I do not know that

women, *as* women, want anything in particular, but as human beings they want, my good men, exactly what you want yourselves: interesting occupation, reasonable freedom for their pleasures, and a sufficient emotional outlet. What form the occupation, the pleasures and the emotion may take, depends entirely upon the individual. You know that this is so with yourselves—why will you not believe that it is so with us?

DOROTHY SAYERS

It is perfectly idiotic to take away a woman's traditional occupations and then complain because she looks for new ones. Every woman is a human being—one cannot repeat that too often—and a human being *must* have occupation, if he or she is not to become a nuisance to the world.

DOROTHY SAYERS

Perhaps it is no wonder that the women were first at the Cradle and last at the Cross. They had never known a man like this Man—there never has been such another. A prophet and teacher who never nagged at them, never flattered or coaxed or patronised; who never made arch jokes about them, never treated them either as "The women, God help us!" or "The ladies, God bless them!"; who rebuked without querulousness and praised without condescension; who took their questions and arguments seriously; who never mapped out their sphere for them, never urged them to be feminine or jeered at them for being female; who had no axe to grind and no uneasy male dignity to defend; who took them as he found them and was completely unself-conscious.

DOROTHY SAYERS

A woman must love and respect herself and must experience the self-esteem that comes from successful achievement. This can, in turn, release her love and creative energies in a new way so that her family and society are benefited rather than hurt. Jesus told us to love our neighbor as ourselves. The woman who is not being true to herself finds it extremely difficult to love herself. Until she learns to do this, she may never know what it really means to love others, even her own family, in spite of all her talk about sacrificing and living for them alone.

LETHA SCANZONI AND NANCY HARDESTY

True worth is in being, not seeming;
    In doing each day that goes by
Some little good—not in the dreaming
    Of great things to do by-and-by.
For whatever men say in blindness,
    And spite of the fancies of youth,
There's nothing so kingly as kindness,
    And nothing so royal as truth.

ALICE CARY

Can one actually find oneself in someone else? In someone else's love? . . . I believe that true identity is found, as Eckhart once said, by "going into one's own ground and knowing one-self." It is found in creative activity springing from within . . . . Woman can best refind herself by losing herself in some kind of creative activity of her own.

ANNE MORROW LINDBERGH

Only the category of personhood is adequate for meeting the needs of women, or of society as a whole. As we cannot afford to squander our natural resources of minerals, food, and beauty, so we cannot afford to discard any human resources of brains, skills, and initiative, even though it is women who possess them.

MARY MCDERMOTT SHIDELER

The Remarkable Lady
of Proverbs Thirty-one

Only she deserves talents who uses them.

The little lady in Proverbs 31 is really quite a gal. Observing all the scope and freedom she had to develop and organize, invest and manage, create and supervise, give love and receive honor, we marvel at her freedom and high status in those Old Testament days. She surely had it better than many Christian women today. Let's take a fresh look at her.

We assume that a man is the author of Proverbs 31. If so, it comes as no surprise that the first thing he mentions is: "Her husband can trust her, and she will richly satisfy his needs" (v. 11 LB). For although sex is but one facet of married life, it is a very important facet, and it is difficult indeed for a marriage to be truly happy and satisfying if the sexual life of the couple is not pleasurable. In this case it would seem that sex for both of them is mutually satisfying. Not only does she richly satisfy his needs, but he satisfies hers too, for how else could he trust her? She feels no need to seek adventure elsewhere. Both he and she are contented and at ease.

Wise woman that she is, however, she knows better than to build their relationship on a sensuous level only. We read, "She will not hinder him, but help him all her life" (v. 12 LB). They pull together. A common goal and purpose knit them together. And the relationship is an enduring one. She does not get tired of working and living alongside him. She continues "all her life."

Her own unique identity she finds, however, not in her harmonious relationship with her husband, but in her own creative activities.

"She finds wool and flax and busily spins it" (v. 13 LB). She becomes, on a small scale, a cloth manufacturer. With loom and spinning wheel she delights to see beautiful yardage whirred off, limited in pattern, color, texture, and design only by her imaginative mind.

"She buys imported foods, brought by ship from distant ports" (v. 14 LB). She is cosmopolitan, not provincial. Not content with just the sauerkraut and pigs feet or meatballs and fruit soup her mother taught her to make, in a spirit of adventure she experiments with curry and rice, chow mein, tacos, enchiladas, shish kabobs, seaweed, octopus, brains, Yorkshire pudding. She is conscious of being part of a wider world, and she wants her children to grow up with this awareness and appreciation also.

"She gets up before dawn to prepare breakfast for her household, and plans the day's work for her servant girls" (v. 15 LB). Absorbed as she is in outside concerns, she still loves her family enough to prepare meals for them—even breakfast. (Friendhubby, who commutes on the freeway and has to leave before dawn, doesn't have to sit on a stool and eat his breakfast in a restaurant. She prepares it . Maybe once in a while, though, she sleeps in?)

Captivated and lured as she is by so many diverse outside interests, wisely she understands she cannot do it all herself. So she uses some of her income to offer a living to others. She utilizes all the aids she can to free her for the work she enjoys and does best.

Evidently she has access to at least some of the family finances and has freedom to do a little investing of her own, for "She goes out to inspect a field, and buys it; with her own hands she plants a vineyard" (v. 16 LB).

No impulse buyer, she carefully looks over the field. It will be a wise investment, she decides. She can see it being turned into a productive vineyard. So she purchases it and begins to plant.

The next comment does not surprise us—we had already

guessed it! "She is energetic, a hard worker" (v. 17 LB).

We suspect, however, that her many-faceted ventures, the prospect of realizing substantial profit, and the immense satisfaction she receives from her work motivate her to work harder than ever and infuse her with boundless energy.

"[She] . . . watches for bargains . . ." (v. 18 LB). Perhaps this is one of the reasons she has money to invest in real estate.

"She sews for the poor, and generously gives to the needy" (vv. 19, 20 LB). In spite of all her business commitments, she has time for volunteer work. And her giving is not only the rather impersonal giving of cash. She invests some of her precious time, too, and with her own hands sews for the poor. But, note, her volunteer work is purposeful and meets basic human needs. It is not simply busywork.

"She has no fear of winter for her household, for she has made warm clothes for all of them" (v. 21 LB). She thinks and plans ahead, forsees and provides for needs before they come, and this frees her from frenzied worry and anxiety.

"She also upholsters with finest tapestry; her own clothing is beautifully made—a purple gown of pure linen" (v. 22 LB).

Remarkable woman! Careful in her money management and concerned about the poor, she still is inwardly free to appreciate, cultivate, and enjoy beauty. Her home is tastefully decorated. She herself is well groomed, a delight to the eyes.

"Her husband is well known, for he sits in the council chamber with the other civic leaders" (v. 23 LB). Her husband's position undoubtedly calls for home entertaining, and she probably accompanies him to social functions. From the profile we already have gleaned of this fantastic lady, we can assume that she is a gracious and poised hostess and quite possibly, because of her varied outside interests, an interesting conversationalist and one who moves with ease in all circles.

"She makes belted linen garments to sell to the merchants" (v. 24 LB). Busy lady that she is, she discovers that she still has a little extra time. Her creative ventures spark more creativity, so she ventures now to open a wholesale clothing manufacturing shop so she can sell brand-name clothes to retailers.

"She is a woman of strength and dignity . . ." (v. 25 LB). She walks tall, not downgrading herself, but accepting her strengths and her value as a unique child of God. She is not weak, helpless, coy, or flirtatious, nor is there any suggestion that she flaunts her femininity. She respects herself and calls forth respect from others.

"She . . . has no fear of old age" (v. 25 LB). Little wonder—young in spirit now, she probably will always be young. Her apparently successful business ventures will assure her of a carefree retirement financially. Also, we are told that one of the predominant psychological needs of old age is to be able to look back on one's life with satisfaction. She surely will be able to do this, for not only has she succeeded in her professional life, but in her personal life as well. We read, "Her children stand and bless her . . ." (v. 28 LB). (Interesting also that this is the first mention of her children. Devoted mother that she is, her children don't dominate her life.)

In spite of all her achievements she has not neglected the care and nurture of her mind. Mental and emotional growth and development are reflected in the words: "When she speaks, her words are wise . . ." (v. 26 LB).

Equally remarkable is the fact that though she has several working under her whom she must supervise, still ". . . kindness is the rule for everything she says" (v. 26 LB).

And though all her business ventures surely must draw her away from home a good bit of the time, still "She watches carefully all that goes on throughout her household, and is never lazy" (v. 27 LB).

She is tuned in to her family and reads the signs when Jimmy comes home from school sullen and aggressive, or Sue locks herself in her room, or friend-husband puffs out his cheeks as he slams the car door shut.

Little wonder her children stand (that is, they objectively observe her) and bless her, and her husband praises her with these words: "There are many fine women in the world, but you are the best of them all!" (v. 29 LB).

Secure man that he is, he is not threatened by this remarkable, aggressive, energetic, astute, brilliant, charming, and compassionate woman who is his wife. Rather, his eyes light up with pride, fondness softens his face when he gazes at her, and he cheers her on, knowing there is no higher motivation than to receive praise.

And so we come at last to those two qualities that today are considered of prime importance if a woman is going to win a Miss America Contest: "Charm can be deceptive and beauty doesn't last . . ." (v. 30 LB). What a switch on values to have these two qualities listed last! Nor is this remarkable woman credited with either.

". . . but a woman who fears and reverences God shall be greatly praised" (v. 30 LB). The crowning attribute of this remarkable woman is that she is a person committed to God. She knows from whence her strengths and abilities come, and she fears and reverences God.

"Praise her for the many fine things she does. These good deeds of hers shall bring her honor and recognition from even the leaders of the nations" (v. 31 LB).

Amazing words! On the basis of these words we can declare that it's all right for a Christian woman to be strong, creative, energetic, innovative, in charge of finances, investing in real estate, working outside the home, devoted to her family, poised, intelligent, dignified, appreciating beauty, daring, adventuresome, cosmopolitan, a caring person, a volunteer worker, and alive sexually (did all her interests contribute to vigor in this area too?) And not only is it all right, but she is to be praised for it—and not only quietly at home by her family, but even the leaders of the nations shall take note and honor her. Her husband receives local civic honor, but she receives national honor. And even with that being the case, she is not considered as being in competition with her husband, nor does he resent it.

Remarkable woman of Proverbs 31, I shake my head and ask, How can all these attributes possibly be wrapped up in one woman? Or are you a composite picture of all the desirable qualities of a wife and mother? Pondering it further, I chuckle to myself and think: Perhaps this is why enterprising men in the Old Testament times took unto themselves several wives, that in the several they might enjoy completeness and wholeness.

But then I wonder if their wives were not a bit cheated? For can any single man hope to be a completely total person any more than any woman? Or is this why this homily is introduced with the question: A good wife who can find? Did the one sketching the profile know his ideal was so lofty no one could find her, yet he couldn't resist dreaming about her? And if this were the case, what insights we receive into the heart of a remarkable man! Fortunate also the woman who finds him!

Whatever the case may be, I confess that, remarkable woman of Proverbs 31, you do inspire, motivate, liberate, and thrill me.

Role Models For Younger Persons

Women today must begin to provide role models for younger women, rather than urging them to simply get a man, get married and beget children. Women now must demonstrate for the next generation that we can be dedicated Christians as well as dedicated competent achievers in the occupational realm. That we can be supportive, loving wives without being subservient, self-denying and destructive. That we can successfully combine love of family, dedication to profession, and discipleship to Christ.

LETHA SCANZONI AND NANCY HARDESTY

Mary, Mother of Jesus, What Can You Teach Me?

The religion of a child depends on what its mother and father *are*, and not only on what they say.

H. F. AMIEL

"The modern woman will note with pleasant surprise that Mary of Nazareth, while completely devoted to the will of God, was far from being a timidly submissive woman . . . . On the contrary, she was a woman who proclaimed that God vindicates the humble and the oppressed and removes the powerful people of this world from their privileged positions," Pope Paul VI wrote in a letter to all Roman Catholic bishops on March 22, 1976.

If we listen to the words of Mary's Magnificat against the backdrop of the conditions of her day, I wonder if we can come to any other conclusion.

The people in Nazareth, Mary's hometown, were extremely poor. Most of them were farmers, trying to eke out sufficient food from minuscule farms they owned or rented from absentee landlords.

Taxes imposed a heavy burden. The Jewish religious leaders not only demanded what was required in the Mosaic Law but went far beyond those requirements. Ten percent of the income of the people was collected for the support of the priests, and there were over six thousand priests in Jerusalem alone! The religious leaders ordered that a tenth of the cattle be given for sacrifices, and every third year they extracted ten percent more—as an offering for the poor, ironically enough. A special tax was inflicted when the first-born child was born.

Herod exacted from the common people a poll tax for the building fund of the temple, and then, since he was an impulse buyer and never had a large enough budget to work with, he slapped on an additional sales tax.

Rome collected export and import taxes. Water tax, property tax, taxes to finance the Roman highways, salt and meat tax—where did it stop? Historians reckon that Mary and Joseph's nation was the most heavily taxed nation the world has ever known.

Small wonder then that most of the people of Nazareth were reduced to living in the caves that pockmarked Nazareth's stony hillsides. When we visited the Holy Land our guide took us to a cave that quite likely was similar to the home it is believed Mary and Joseph lived in.

We entered through a winding passageway. We peered down into a hole chiseled out of soft limestone on the right side.

"A cistern for storing water," our guide explained.

On the left we discovered a similar hole.

"For storing grain," our guide added.

The room we entered was about twelve feet by eight and a half and about six feet high. A small hole in the ceiling filtered in air and light from outside.

"Did they have any furniture?" I asked.

Our guide shrugged. "Joseph was a carpenter, so yes, perhaps they had a table. Others would tip a bushel basket upside down and use it as a table. Would they have chairs? That's questionable. They would have a chest in which to store the family records, a spinning wheel, a loom. That's about all."

I looked at the bare little stone cave room. Old familiar verses took on new meaning: ". . . [Jesus] did not count equality with God a thing to be grasped, but emptied himself, taking the form of a servant . . ." (Philippians 2:6, 7 RSV). ". . . though he was rich, yet for your sake he became poor . . ." (2 Corinthians 8:9 RSV).

And poverty is never nice, I thought. I had witnessed enough of it among the people of India during the seven years I lived there.

Poverty means fighting dirt and being dirty because soap costs money, and there isn't money even for soap. Poverty means not being able to sleep at night, because you shiver with cold. Poverty means being sick often and nursing sick, whining babies, many of whom will never survive and grow into adulthood because of malnutrition. Poverty means bodies infested with intestinal parasites: roundworms, pinworms, tapeworms. Poverty means being crowded and no one in the family ever having privacy. Poverty robs the sparkle from the eye, the life from the step, the lilt from the voice, the hope from the heart, and the song from the throat.

All these thoughts were tumbling about in my mind as we walked out from the cave, so I almost stumbled over the six-inch-high threshold.

"Careful!" cautioned our guide, and then he went on to explain the reason for the ledge. In Nazareth garbage was thrown into the streets for the scavenger birds, dogs, cats, rats, and chickens to devour. When a torrent of rain pelted the town, the streets became canals, awash with floating garbage. The ledge at the entryway was to keep the putrefying garbage from pouring into the cave.

I thought of the streets of Calcutta and the open sewers overflowing in the monsoons, and I felt my nose twitch.

"And, of course," our guide continued, "with garbage, you always get flies." He chuckled. "Flies must be some of the world's most prolific reproducers. A female lays 130 eggs in one batch and she may lay from 2 to 21 batches during her lifetime. One housefly lays so many eggs that a scientist named Hodge figured that if a pair of flies mated in April and all their descendants lived, the flies of this one family would cover the earth forty-seven feet deep by August."

I shuddered. Flies had plagued us in East Africa. Sticky, lazy creatures, two or three dozen would often settle on our backs as a black cloud and ride along as we walked. Out-of-doors we spoke with care, for if we opened our mouths too wide, a fly might zoom in. And we often saw African children with flies crawling all over their lips and up their nostrils.

"The Jews hated the flies too," our guide said. "That's why

they nicknamed Satan, *Beelzebub,* which means, 'lord of the flies.' "

The picture of the little home in Nazareth which my Sunday school take-home papers had bequeathed me in my childhood was fast crumbling. Those pictures had shown Mary, prettily garbed (always in blue), sitting at her loom. Joseph was busy with his saw. The angelic-looking Christ child played happily. Flowers trailed up the walls of the house. Birds sang in the trees. Green grass spread a velvety carpet underneath. It all looked so pretty and peaceful and nice. Unconsciously whenever I had looked at the picture I felt good that it had all been so nice for Jesus when He came to earth. Now I was beginning to suspect that even in His childhood and youth maybe He hadn't had it so nice after all.

We know the people of Nazareth had grown restive in their poverty, partly because they had occasion to see the wealth of the few and contrast it with their poverty. The trade routes of those days brought some of the wealth into view, and Nazareth lay in a position where important trade routes ran either through the city or close to it.

The trade routes were the freeways of that day, slower moving but more colorful. Camels ambled along, protesting raucously under their loads. Donkeys with bulging baggage brayed. Dark-skinned porters, bearing colorful sedan chairs on poles on their shoulders, ran, panting and perspiring. From behind the curtains of those sedan chairs rouged, mascaraed, and heavily perfumed wealthy Greek women peered out. Opulent Eastern merchants, swathed in long, white robes, alternately walked or, sitting astride camels, swayed from side to side and back and forth. Scattered here and there among the crowd would be sandal-shod Jewish pilgrims, clad in rough homespun, headed for Jerusalem.

As children Mary and Joseph very likely sat on Nazareth's hillsides and watched the caravans passing on the trade routes below. Even as disadvantaged people today, reading or learning about the wealth of others, grow restive, rebellious, and resentful, surely Mary and Joseph too must have experienced these feelings.

View Mary's Magnificat with new insight and hear the cries of a young revolutionary, the cries of an adolescent deeply concerned about human justice:

. . . My soul magnifies the Lord,
and my spirit rejoices in God my Savior,
for he has regarded the low estate of his handmaiden . . . .
He has shown strength with his arm,
he has scattered the proud in the imagination of their hearts,
he has put down the mighty from their thrones,
and exalted those of low degree;
he has filled the hungry with good things,
and the rich he has sent empty away.

Luke 1:46–48, 51–53 RSV

I find it significant that when God chose a woman to be mother of His Son, He chose one who was concerned about the social injustices of her day.

Mary also was a woman of supreme faith. Our guide led us to a second cave which traditionally is called the cave of the annunciation. This cave boasts two small rooms. Over the arched entryway to the second room a simple sign declares: HERE GOD BECAME FLESH.

The words so staggered my mind as I read them that I collapsed on the stone bench in the first room and asked my family if I could be alone for a few moments.

What human mind can comprehend that He who is Creator and Upholder of the Universe was willing to lose His identity—painful experience that that is—and to abandon whatever form He had at that time to become an egg, swimming in the ocean of a woman's womb, hidden for nine months? And what mind can comprehend what it must have been for the woman to be told that this could happen to her?

Mary was an active participant in this venture. No place do we read that she asked leave to run to Joseph and ask his permission first. God spoke directly to her, and she answered directly. Her words were simple but magnificent words of faith as befits all profound experiences: ". . . let it be . . . !" The fact that she really did believe that it had been accomplished is reflected in Elizabeth's word of greeting to her later: "And blessed is she *who believed* that there would be a fulfilment of what was spoken to her from the Lord" (Luke 1:45 RSV, italics added). Mary, mother of Jesus, how staggering your faith is! How you challenge me!

Mary was yielded to God. She responds ". . . Behold, I am the handmaid of the Lord; let it be to me according to your word" (Luke 1:38 RSV).

I wonder what lies behind those words. I can only guess.

The Jews of Mary's day believed the Messiah would come to free them from their grinding poverty and to usher in reform. Did Mary's thirst for justice for her people so consume her that she exulted now in the fact that she, yes, *she* would be used of God to bring this to pass? Do we find in her exclamation, ". . . let it be to me according to your word" more awed realization and glad acceptance than mere humble acquiescing resignation?

We already have caught glimpses of Mary's fervor for social justice in her Magnificat. Some Bible scholars believe that James, the author of the earthy, I-want-to-see-proof-of-your-faith letter which bears his name, was a brother of Jesus. If this is so, do we not see reflected in that vigorous, no-nonsense epistle some of the convictions Mary deeply believed in, talked about in her home, and quite likely passed on to her children? If this epistle then reflects some of Mary's feelings, and if her expectation was that the Messiah would correct the injustices of her day, can we not hear in her ". . . let it be to me!" eager, overjoyed expectation, awe and wonder? And could not this certainty that she had been caught up into the stream of God's purposes equip, fortify, and strengthen her for the testings that lay ahead?

I have a dear eighty-two-year-old friend, Mary Helmke, who has this strong sense of living and moving in partnership with God. Mary greets her Lord every morning with these words: "Good Morning, Father. This is your child, Mary, checking in. What do you have for me to do today? I am available."

Those of us who know Mary marvel at all God finds for an eighty-two-year-old lady to do.

When I have related Mary's greeting to women whom I address at meetings, not a few have confided afterwards how hesitant they would be to pray this just one day! And one lady who did get courage to pray it, found the Lord engineering the events of that day in such a way that it resulted in many months of her concerned care for some of God's children in need. "And I wouldn't have missed it for anything!" she declared.

Mary, mother of Jesus, your implicit trust in your God which enabled you to yield gladly, recklessly, and unreservedly, coaxes me to trust my God more.

Mary also was a person of trust. Trust differs from faith. Mary believed that she had already become the mother of God's Son. But she needed huge chunks of trust for the testings that followed. How was she going to explain all this to Joseph? Surely she and Elizabeth discussed this when Mary went to visit her aged cousin soon after the angel's visit. It would seem that they came to the conclusion that they must trust God to work it out, for nowhere do we read of Mary trying to defend herself or explain her situation. This implicit trust that God would work things out must have been all the more difficult, because Mary knew the three courses of action that were open to Joseph.

He could divorce her publicly, appearing before the elders and declaring the child was not his—which was true. The sentence would be pronounced: adulteress—the penalty: stoning. The judges would drag Mary to one of the hills of Nazareth and tell her to jump. If she did not, they would push her from the cliff. Then they would watch to see if the body below stirred. If it did, they would pick up stones to fling at it until it stirred no more.

Or Joseph could give her a purse of money and send her far away with orders never to return. Think what a terrifying prospect this would be for a pregnant, teenage, unmarried girl!

The last alternative would be for Joseph to swallow his pride, pretend the child was his, ignore the wagging tongues of the women and the joshing of the men and terminate the marriage as quickly as possible.

We know that Joseph had thought to send her away quietly. Had he actually mentioned this to Mary? If so, what sleepless nights must have followed for her, what pleading with God, what throwing of herself upon His mercy!

Mary, mother of Jesus, when I face difficult, dark days, when I see no way out, I can remember you and your trust and be strengthened in my faith.

Mary, like most other mothers, sometimes couldn't understand her son. She couldn't understand why He stayed behind in the temple and caused them so much anxiety. Surely she must have wondered when He, the oldest son, who should have cared for the family [historians think Joseph had died, for he is not mentioned after the pilgrimage to Jerusalem] announced that He was leaving home to become a vagrant evangelist—without a salary or a supporting congregation! And if, as we think, Mary, like many others of her time, anticipated that the Messiah would be one who would set up an earthly kingdom and alleviate the living conditions of her people, how puzzling then to have Jesus speak, instead, of being killed. And consider her hurt the day He refused to see her, but cried out to the crowd, instead, that His mother, His brothers, and His sisters were those who did the will of God! Not only did He seem to be denying His kinship with her, but He also seemed to be implying that she was opposing God. This was, of course, true at this time, because it would seem that Mary and His family were seeking to bring Jesus home, where they undoubtedly would have tried to dissuade Him from following the course He was on, one that seemed as if it would end only in tragedy. It is even possible that Mary thought her son was going mad—a number of His friends had expressed their concern. And how immense must have been Mary's perplexity and despair when Jesus finally was killed—and as a criminal!

Mary, mother of Jesus, I see in your experience the common experience of all mothers. Often we do not understand our children, but we know we must let them go. And remembering that your son also is God, we share with you the experience of often having God deal with us in ways we cannot understand.

But over and over Mary experienced God working in her behalf. While Joseph was sleeping, God sent an angel to tell Joseph to take Mary as his wife, not to send her away. What an answer to prayer this was for Mary!

I wonder too, did Mary, from the reading of the Scriptures in the synagogue, know of the prophecy that the Messiah was to be born in Bethlehem? Did she, then, see in the decree for enrollment from Herod, the ordering of events by God so she would have to go to Bethlehem for the birth of her child? Was it this conviction also that prevented her from stopping at the home of Elizabeth, her cousin, when she undoubtedly already was in labor on the last lap of their journey to Bethlehem and the most natural thing would have been to stop at the house of a relative?

And was the choral chanting of the heavenly host not only for the shepherds, but also for Mary? In Mary's day it was customary for the girl friends and relatives of the new mother to come to the home after the birth of a child, encircle it, and sing. In the Bethlehem stable, miles and miles away from Nazareth and family and friends, is it not possible that Mary felt lonely because her friends could not share their new-found joy, and that she thought wistfully that she was missing out on having them sing for her? Did our Father-God, who tells us His care is so tender that He notes every sparrow that falls to the ground, understand this human longing of this new mother, and make up for it by arranging for a whole host of heavenly beings to chant praises and celebrate Mary's son's birth?

We visited Bethlehem twice. It is believed that the cave where Mary lay that night was on the side of the hill which drops down to a small plateau known as the Shepherd's Field. As we stood looking down at the Shepherd's Field that day, which is the site of a boys' school today, we could see the boys playing on the field below.

"How big is a host?" I asked my husband.

"No one knows for sure," he said, "but it denotes a very large group indeed—a multitude."

"I wonder then," I said, thinking out loud, "if it was possible that Mary, in the stable here on the hillside, heard the heavenly host chanting praise to God and recognized in this choir God's substitute for the singing of her girl friends had she been in Nazareth."

Possible? I think so, for over and over in life I have noticed God bringing "extra" blessings and joys into my life, over and above my needs, to cheer and encourage me and to say to me, "I love you—extravagantly, and I care about your most personal needs."

Later in life Mary saw her son provide for the needs at the wedding at Cana. She saw Him healing innumerable hurting people. She heard Him provide for her care while He was dying on the cross. And she lived to see Him resurrected, to understand who He is and what His purpose is and to see the Church founded.

Deeply concerned about the social injustices of her day, Mary entrusted her concern to God and let Him direct her as to how this concern could best be expressed. From her came two sons (possibly more also, but we shall consider only two here). One, the divine Son of God, declared at the beginning of His ministry:

The Spirit of the Lord is upon me,
　　because he has anointed me to preach good news to the poor.
He has sent me to proclaim release to the captives
　　　and recovering of sight to the blind,
to set at liberty those who are oppressed,
to proclaim the acceptable year of the Lord.

Luke 4:18, 19, RSV.

By His teaching and through His life this son demonstrated His concern for the spiritual, physical, and social good of the people.

Mary's second son, James (if the scholars are correct in assuming that James indeed was a brother of Jesus), left to the Christian world perhaps the most forthright and peppery declaration that we have proclaiming that God's people must be concerned about social injustices if men are to believe their Christian faith is valid. Consider but one statement of his:

　　My brothers! What good is it for a man to say, "I have faith," if his actions do not prove it? Can that faith save him? Suppose there are brothers or sisters who need clothes and don't have enough to eat. What good is there in your saying to them, "God bless you! Keep warm and eat well!"—if you don't give them the necessities of life? This is how it is with faith: if it is alone and has no actions with it, then it is dead.

James 2:14–17 TEV

Thus, under God's guidance, as she was willing to yield to Him, trust Him and risk all, even when she could not understand what God was doing, Mary was able to actualize a concern for her fellowman that has been universally heard down through the centuries.

Mary, mother of Jesus, you encourage me to trust God wholeheartedly to lead and direct me too, so the concerns of my heart may be most fully realized.

Pondering it all, I, a twentieth-century mother, ask myself:

Do I share Mary's concern about poverty and social injustice?

For what particular thing is God asking me to have faith in Him now?

Can I trust my Lord enough to give Him *all* of me?

When has Jesus dealt with me in such a way that I have not been sure what He is doing? Have I been able to trust Him then? What has been my response?

How have I seen God work on my behalf in my life?

God, I thank You for Mary, mother of Jesus.

. . . our biggest problem is not the submission of one sex to the domination of the other. Our biggest problem is a society so totally preoccupied with individual "rights" that *none of us*—male or female—seems able to make that preliminary and ongoing total submission to *God* from which all other acts of submission and authority must be derived if they are not to become corrupt and idolatrous. The servant and the master, the husband and the wife, the parent and the child, the teacher and the student, the pastor and the parishioner all serve the same Master, and it is only as we are first individually committed to *him* that we can be trusted not to make idols of ourselves in positions of authority, or idols of our masters in positions of submission.

DR. V. MARY STEWART

The Bible constantly reverberates with the twin themes of self-hood and self-loss, and makes it clear that only in Christ is this paradox resolved. If, as a man or a woman, I insist on my self-hood through any other route but that of self-effacing servanthood before God and my brothers and sisters, then I will end up with a false and unhappy self, incapable of either true leadership or true submission. But the opposite is also true: if, as a man or a woman, I think I can *avoid* learning who I am and what my calling is before God simply by doing what everyone else thinks I should do—then I have equally lost the possibility of knowing either true leadership or true submission. Far too many men in the church have made the first mistake; far too many women have made the second.

DR. V. MARY STEWART

Set Me Free, Lord

Set me free, O Lord, from fear
  of having my children grow away from me,
  of opening myself to someone and not being understood,
  of pain,
  of having the children leave home,
    my husband die,

and I myself growing old.
Set me free, O Lord, from habitually
    complaining instead of being grateful,
    envying others and downgrading myself,
    criticizing instead of affirming my loved ones,
    and spooning self-pity all over myself.
Set me free, O Lord, from
    lackadaisical living,
    introverted interests,
    provincial perspectives,
    slovenly sloth,
    and smug satisfaction.
Set me free, O Lord, instead
    to praise,
    glorify,
    worship,
    thank, and adore You—
and to live out that praise in my daily life.

The Faith of a Mother—
Monica, Mother of Augustine

Why has our sincere prayer for each other such great power over others? Because of the fact that by cleaving to God during prayer I become one spirit with Him, and unite with myself by faith and love, those for whom I pray, for the Holy Ghost acting in me, also acts at the same time in them, for He accomplishes all things.

JOHN OF CRONSTADT

Augustine, who lived between 354 and 430, was bishop of Hippo. He was born in Algeria, Africa, the son of a pagan father and a Christian mother. A playboy in youth, Augustine at twenty-nine began to search for wisdom. At thirty-three he was baptized as a Christian and gave his time and energy from that time on to developing and nurturing the Christian community. The following accounts are from *Love Song*, Sherwood Wirt's translation of *Augustine's Confessions*. In these accounts Augustine describes his relationship with his mother, Monica.

During my sixteenth year the thorny branches of sex and temptation trapped me in a briar patch that grew over my head . . . . Oh, me! I don't suppose I dare claim that you had nothing to say, my God, while I kept wandering farther from you. Were you really silent? Whose words were they that my mother, your faithful one, kept sounding in my ears, if they weren't yours? Not that any of them ever reached my heart or had any effect on me. I remember her counseling me privately and expressing her deep concern that I should not indulge in fornication, and especially that I should never commit adultery with another's wife. But it sounded to me like female talk and to conform to it would have made me blush.

Of course they were your words, but I didn't know it. I thought you were mute and she was doing the talking, but now I know you were not silent, but were speaking to me through her. So when her advice was rejected it meant you were being despised by me—by me, her son, the son of your handmaid, your servant. But I didn't know, and went blindly on my headlong course. I was ashamed to be less scandalous than my friends, whom I heard bragging about their disgusting exploits; and the more disgusting the episodes were, the more they bragged about them. So I did the same things they did, not simply for the pleasure of doing them, but mostly for the praise I hoped to get . . . .

My mother was aware that my sexual drives were creating problems for me and were full of dangerous possibilities for the future, but she didn't think it wise at the time to put them on leash within the bounds of married love (assuming they could not be cut back to the quick). My mother took no action because she was afraid that a wife would be a hindrance and stumbling block to my career—not to those hopes of a future life which she had in you, Lord, but to her hopes for me academically.

Both my parents were very much concerned about my studies—my father because he almost never thought about you and had shallow enough thoughts about me; my mother because she judged that the normal course of my studies would be no personal detriment, but could very well help me to find you. To the best of my recollection, that's the way I interpret the inclination of my parents at the time. In any case I was free to do as I liked without proper restraints, and so fell into loose habits and got generally knocked about. And in all of this, my God, a heavy mist shut off my view of the brightness of your truth, while my sins ballooned out in fatness.

[Years intervene, then the story continues.]

Then you stretched forth your hand from above and drew up my soul from the dark abyss. That faithful servant of yours, my mother, came to you in my behalf with more tears than most mothers shed at a child's funeral. Her faith in you had made plain to her that I was spiritually dead. And you heard her, Lord, you heard her. You didn't ignore the tears that fell from her eyes and watered the earth everywhere she prayed. You heard her and sent her a dream that so relieved her mind that she allowed me to live with her and to eat at the same table in the house. That was something she had refused to permit for some time because she so loathed the blasphemy and error in which I was swimming.

In her dream she saw herself standing on a kind of measuring rule or wooden yardstick, wailing and overcome with grief. A radiant young man approached her in a happy and laughing mood and asked her the reason for all this protracted weeping. (His purpose was not to learn from her but to teach her, as is customary in such dreams.) She replied that she was mourning the ruin of my soul. He then admonished her and, in a reassuring way, ordered her to look more carefully and she would see that I was standing precisely where she was. When she did look, she saw me standing next to her on the same measuring rule. Where did this dream come from if you, Lord, did not "cause your ear to hear" and so prepare her heart? O you Omnipotent Goodness, you care for us all as if each of us were your only concern, and you look after each of us as if we were all one person!

When Mother told me about her dream, I tried to disparage it, saying I interpreted it to mean she shouldn't give up hope, because one day she would be as I was [a Manichean]. She, however, came back at me immediately, saying, "No, it was not told me, 'Where he is, there you will be,' but rather, 'Where you are, there he will be.' " And this too I take to have come from you. I confess to you, Lord, that to the best of my memory your answer which you gave through my mother impressed me more than the dream itself. She was not disturbed by my misinterpretation, because she had quickly grasped the meaning of the dream, which I had not seen until she spoke. So the joy that was to come to that godly woman years later was predicted as a consolation for the anguish I was causing her at the time.

Nearly nine years were to pass during which I sank deeper into the mire and false darkness. I tried to climb out, but each time I fell backward and sprawled in the muck. And all the while this devout, gentle, modest widow (and such you love) was heartened by this hope. She never stopped her sighing and weeping; she never stopped beseeching you at all hours of the day and night, pounding away on my behalf before your presence. I know her prayers came before you, and yet you still abandoned me to the pitch and roll of the darkness.

I remember one other answer to prayer that you gave my mother. You gave it to her through your holy servant, a certain bishop who had been brought up in the church and was well trained in your Scriptures. This woman, my mother, went to him and asked if he would please have a talk with me. She wanted him to refute my errors, to show me where I was mixed up in my thinking, and so set me straight. It seems he often did this when he found the kind of people who were open to receive his instruction.

However, the bishop refused to see me—very wisely, as I later came to believe. He told her that at that time I was unteachable because I was all puffed up with the novelty of my weird ideas, and that I had already harassed and upset a number of immature persons with my questions, as she had indicated to him. "But," he said, "let him alone. Just keep praying to the Lord for him. He will discover through his reading what his error is, and how God looks at it." At the same time he went on to tell her that his own mother had been a Christian but she had been subverted by the Manicheans while he was still young. Not only had he read practically all the Manicheans' books, he had actually copied them out. Then he had come to the realization, without debate or argument with anyone else, that he would have to leave the sect; so he left it. After he said this to my mother, she was still not satisfied; she kept crying and pleading all the more, asking him to see me and talk with me. Finally he became weary and irritated with her and said,

"Now go. As sure as you are alive, it is not possible that the son of these tears should be lost." As she often told me afterward, she accepted the answer as if it were a voice from heaven.

[Years pass, and then we take up Augustine's account again.]

Mother had come to join me in Milan. Her love had given her the courage to cross land and sea, and when she found herself in danger she simply sought her safety in you. On one occasion as the ship on which she was crossing from Africa seemed about to sink, it was she who put valor into the hearts of the sailors rather than vice versa. She told them there was no question that they would land safely, because you had promised it to her in a vision—and they did.

When Mother reached Milan I informed her that while I was not a Christian, neither was I any longer a Manichean. She seemed unimpressed. Quietly she witnessed to me out of a confident heart of her faith in Christ, and predicted that before she left this life she would see me a believer.

[Again there is an interval of time.]

Every effort was being made to find me a wife. I proposed to a girl and accordingly we became engaged. My mother did all she could to bring off the marriage, because she reasoned that the wedding would be followed by my baptism. She saw this as the answer to her prayers. The plans went forward, and the arrangement was made for marriage to this girl who was two years under the legal age. I liked her all right and agreed to wait for her.

Meanwhile my sins kept on multiplying. The woman who shared my bed for so many years was torn from my side as an "impediment" to my forthcoming marriage; but my heart, broken and bleeding, still clung to her. She sailed back to Africa . . . leaving me with our natural son. I was impatient at the prospect of a two-year delay before I could marry my intended wife, and being a slave to sex rather than a lover of marriage, I acquired another unattached female.

[There is another interlude of time. During this period Augustine, following the hearing of a number of lectures and contacts with a number of Christians, is brought into his final conflict with God. He experiences an immense struggle of his will, but at long last he is enabled to turn himself over to God.]

We went into the house and gave my mother the news and she was overjoyed. When we explained to her how it had all come about, she was exuberant and triumphant and gave thanks to you who are "able to do far more abundantly than all that we ask or think." She saw that you had given her, on my behalf, far more than she was used to asking for in all her sobbings and groanings and wailings. You had converted me to yourself on the same rule of faith you had revealed to her so many years before, and had turned all her mourning into gladness.

Questions to Ponder

In what ways had Monica contributed to her son's waywardness? Do you think this accentuated her grief over the life he was living? Why?

How did Monica demonstrate her love for her wayward son? What did she have to accept?

What would you say were some of Monica's strongest points? What were her weakest points?

Later in life she seems to have passed into a more tranquil state of faith regarding the final outcome for her son. What do you think contributed to this?

To Many Parents

Christ saw her weeping for her son,
The widow who had no other.
At once the healing work was done:
He delivered him to his mother.

Christ heard him pleading for his son
With hope—with longing, rather.
At once the healing work was done:
He delivered him to his father.

Oh, you with children lost awhile,
Some morning fresh and new,
Our Lord will, with his tenderest smile,
Deliver them to you.

JANE MERCHANT

The here, the now, and the individual, have always been the special concern of the saint, the artist, the poet, and—from time immemorial—the woman. In the small circle of the home she has never quite forgotten the particular uniqueness of each member of the family, the spontaneity of now, the vividness of here. This is the basic substance of life.

ANNE MORROW LINDBERGH

The three best gifts that a child could be born with, says Emmet Fox, in one of his books, are "a good constitution, a good disposition, and horse sense." I'd like to add one more: a sense of humor. If we're lucky enough to receive these gifts as a child, and later as a parent to pass them on, we are indeed blessed in "child rearing."

MARY MARTIN

When the Baby Came

So when the tiny miracle
Was hers, she gasped at all details:
The perfect eyes, and nose, and ears,
The perfectly formed fingernails.

She never tired of marveling
At this, God's tiny bit of news;
And oh! what tracks across her heart
Are made by those size zero shoes!

BARBARA A. JONES

The Baby

The mother left the carriage for a minute, and I went over to
    meet the Holy Trinity living in the baby's pure soul.
It was asleep, its arms carelessly laid on the embroidered sheet.
Its closed eyes looked inward and its chest gently rose and fell
As if to murmur: This dwelling is inhabited.

Lord, you are there.

I adore you in this little one who has not yet disfigured you.
Help me to become like him once more,
To recapture your likeness and your life now so deeply buried
    in my heart.

MICHEL QUOIST

On Children

Your children are not your children.
They are the sons and daughters of Life's longing for
    itself . . . .
You may give them your love but not your thoughts,
For they have their own thoughts.
You may house their bodies but not their souls,
For their souls dwell in the house of tomorrow, which you
    cannot visit, not even in your dreams . . . .
You are the bows from which your children as living arrows are
    sent forth . . . .
Let your bending in the archer's hand be for gladness;
For even as He loves the arrow that flies, so He loves also the
    bow that is stable.

KAHLIL GIBRAN

The joys of motherhood are not fully experienced until all the
children are in bed asleep.

Guidelines for Mothers of Two- and Three-year-olds

The mistakes we make are not nearly as powerful as the love we give our children.

REUEL HOWE

Researchers at the Harvard University Laboratory of Human Development have suggested eight "do's" and twelve "don'ts" for parents of two- and three-year-olds.

1. When the child wants attention the parent should pay attention. If the request is reasonable, grant it.
2. Seek to understand what the child is trying to do.
3. Have a few rules and enforce them. Don't let the child badger you into giving in if the requests are not reasonable.
4. Be generous with encouragement and enthusiasm and provide help when needed.
5. Converse with the child.
6. Be simple and clear in your language but occasionally introduce new words.
7. After a child's needs are satisfied, leave him on his own again.
8. Encourage imaginative play.

The list of practices for mothers to avoid which the researchers suggested was:

1. Don't confine the child in playpen, crib, or yard for long periods, especially if the child wants to get out.

2. Don't be your child's only friend so he becomes glued to you. Provide playmates.
3. Don't make it necessary for your child to throw a tantrum in order to get your attention.
4. Don't be afraid to say "no." Your child will still love you.
5. Don't argue with a child. You speak from different perspectives.
6. Don't worry if your house is cluttered. It's a sign of a healthy, inquisitive child.
7. Don't overprotect your child. Give the explorer a little freedom as long as the adventures are safe.
8. Don't take a full-time job outside the home before your child is in school. Small children need the love and security of one parent with them.
9. Don't dominate your child. Give opportunity for development of uniqueness.
10. Avoid boring situations for your child if possible.
11. Don't be concerned about how soon your child is toilet trained, learns to read, count, and so forth. Some are slow learners but catch up later.
12. Don't make your child feel he is more important than he is. In other words, don't spoil him.

Children Live What They Learn

If a child lives with criticism,
   He learns to condemn.
If a child lives with hostility,
   He learns to fight.
If a child lives with ridicule,
   He learns to be shy.
If a child lives with shame,
   He learns to feel guilty.
If a child lives with tolerance,
   He learns to be patient.

If a child lives with encouragement,
    He learns confidence.
If a child lives with praise,
    He learns to appreciate.
If a child lives with fairness,
    He learns justice.
If a child lives with security,
    He learns to have faith.
If a child lives with approval,
    He learns to like himself.
If a child lives with acceptance and friendship,
    He learns to find love in the world.

AUTHOR UNKNOWN

How to Provide for Emotional Well-being in Your Children

But every home where Love abides
And Friendship is a guest,
Is surely home, and home sweet home,
For there the heart can rest.

HENRY VAN DYKE

Provide a stable home. Broken homes are responsible for 80 percent of America's troubled children. But if your home already is a broken home, there is still lots of hope. You, along with other parents, can follow the remaining guidelines.

Define your goals for your children. What do you want for your children? Do you want them to become gracious, poised, social persons; those who care for people and help them; those who place God first in their lives; parents who provide a good living for their families; citizens who serve their country?

Be positive and full of faith as you pray for your children. Have mental pictures of the kind of persons you want them to become. Thank God they will be like that.

Seek to bring your children into a conscious, personal relationship with God. Make their Christian education not the formal one-hour-only-Sunday-morning kind, but the twenty-four-hour-a-day, unconsciously-rubbing-off-you-onto-them kind. This means *you* have to continue growing.

Invest time and interest in your children. Giving spending money, gifts, treats, or even cultural advantages is no substitute for giving your children time.

"I wish my Dad would go fishing with me once in a while, and I wish my mom wouldn't have to work so hard that she's always tired," Randy, a sensitive, shy teenager wrote on a questionnaire. And then Randy's mother complains that Randy is quarrelsome, restless, hard to live with, and not doing well at school.

In addition to having time for your children in daily living, don't minimize the importance and value of taking time for family vacations and fun outings together. And if there are several children in the family, try to be with each child alone from time to time.

But it isn't only time, it's *interest* in the child that is important. Try to understand what is important to your child and contribute along that line. In this way you relate and communicate.

Ruth Graham, wife of the evangelist, tells of first confiscating her son's rock records, then purchasing new ones and sitting and listening to them with him.

Keep in touch with your children's teachers. Teachers see your children in a different light than you do. Believe what they tell you.

Harry, at twelve, was brushing with the law. "We tried to tell his parents two or three years ago that Harry needed help," one of his teachers told the counselor at the juvenile home where Harry finally landed. "But his parents only defended and excused him."

At the same time, don't turn over to the schools—or the church—the responsibility of rearing your children. If you are a parent, this is your first responsibility.

Know your children's friends.

"Gordon never brought his friends home," Mrs. Seegar said, talking about her second son's venture into the drug world. "His older brother, Tom, did, but not Gordon. Tom used to tell me that Gordon's friends at school were not desirable. But I guess we didn't take it seriously. When we discovered Gordon was on drugs, we found that one of his friends had introduced him to them."

Teach your children to select friends wisely, a family counselor urges. "Choose your place of residence and your church home so good friends will be available. The influence of the peer group today is as great as the home influence."

Listen to your children. Ruth Graham, speaking at a women's convention in Anaheim, California, underscored the need for parents to change their role when children become teenagers. "Talk little. Listen much," she urged. She asked one of her own teenagers how much talking was too much. "Saying the same thing twice," was the reply.

True listening involves putting up all the antennae and trying to understand what the young person is *really* saying—which can be different from the actual words uttered. Don't miss the little clues dropped. Listen with eyes and intuition as well as ears.

Have some restrictions. Have you ever experienced the uneasy and uncomfortable feeling that comes with driving on a new three- or four-lane freeway before the white lines have been painted? Or have you thought what it would be like to drive on city streets without signal lights or stop signs? In the same way children need to have some rules and then have them *enforced.*

If there is willful, deliberate sin, deal with it. Differentiate between sin and accidents or foolish mistakes due to immature judgment. But if you have examined the situation, and there is willful sin, it must be openly dealt with. Don't gloss over "little lies," or "little thefts."

When Jim was eight he started to steal money at home. Then he took from his offering envelopes for church. His parents couldn't believe it was serious. When he was twelve he was shoplifting. At sixteen he stole a car. His father was so angry he told him never to come home again.

So deal with sin *at once.* Drastically, but not hysterically. Let the discipline hurt. This does not necessarily mean physical hurt. Twelve-year-old Scott's stepfather believed, "There is nothing a good slap on the head won't cure." It hasn't cured Scott. He's on probation from Juvenile Hall. Discipline should be commensurate with the misdeed, administered wisely, and aimed at correcting, not punishing.

Don't forget the gospel of forgiveness. As a parent-priest declare to your penitent child that God has forgiven him. Follow up the declaration with a hug and kiss.

All behavior is caused, so try to understand why your child acts as he does. Chronic diarrhea sapped the strength of Sonja, a sensitive, brilliant ten-year-old. Though she qualified for accelerated classes, she had chosen to remain in the regular classes and was failing there too. At home she spent long hours in her bedroom with her door shut. "You didn't do me a favor borning me," she told her mother one day.

The counselor, in talking with Sonja, discovered that her mother and father were quarreling constantly. After years of silent endurance of her husband's violent temper outbursts, Sonja's mother was crying out that she could bear no more. Sonja was knotted with fear that her parents would separate. Sonja's parents had to seek help if they wanted their daughter saved.

Periodically stop and reexamine your goals, ideals, and values. Write down in descending order what you consider most important for yourself and your family. Then evaluate your life as you are living it. Periodic reexamination is needed because unwittingly we can get pulled away from our original intentions.

Offer guidance. Don't just tell your child to work. Work along with him. Enjoy his company. Show him how to do a job properly. In giving vocational guidance, respect your child's wishes, but guide him to sources that can help parents and child together to come to a wise decision.

Give praise and affection. Praise, encourage, and reward your child when you honestly can do so: with a word, a smile, a treat, a trip to the ball game, home-baked bread. Whatever your child enjoys most.

Children also need affection. In a home for troubled children I noticed how the children craved affection. Boys would come up and drape their arms around the necks of counselors or lean on them or punch them in the back as they passed. The counselors were generous in response. A favorite embrace seemed to be to encircle the boy's head with the arm, hold the head close to the body, and then tousle the boy's hair. The boys seemed to enjoy it and did not struggle to be free.

Now if all this seems tedious and perhaps even a bit artificial, perhaps it will help to summarize it in the words of Margaret Boston. Margaret cares for seventy children in Orange County's Albert Sitton Home in California. When I talked with Margaret, she said, "Care for the children, just care for them and about them."

"But surely you must have more to add." I persisted.

"No," she said stubbornly. "Care—really care—for your children, and all the rest will fall naturally into line."

Perhaps that's why the apostle Paul declared, "Love never fails."

Preceding material originally published under the title "What to Do About Troubled Children." Reprinted by permission of ETERNITY Magazine, Copyright 1973, Evangelical Ministries, 1716 Spruce Street, Philadelphia, PA. 19103.

Time Alone for Each Child

"If only, I think," Anne Morrow Lindbergh writes in her classic, *Gifts from the Sea*, "if only we could have each of our children alone, not just for part of each day, but for part of each month, each year. Would they not be happier, stronger, and in the end, more independent because more secure?"

Susanna Wesley taught her children at home, six hours every day with the exception of Sunday. In addition she scheduled private one-hour talks with the children on a rotating basis.

"On Monday, I talk with Molly; on Tuesday, with Hetty; Wednesday, with Nancy; Thursday, with Jacky [John]; Friday, with Patty; Saturday, with Charles; and with Emily and Sukey together, on Sunday."

Lest we think that it was possible for Susanna Wesley because she lived in a slower-moving era containing less activity to compete with, consider the example of Jim and Jo Seeley.

Jim and Jo Seeley of Alexandria, Virginia, have ten children, four of them adopted. The Seeleys give priority to spending time alone with each child every day. From 7:P.M to 10:00 P.M. each parent takes about fifteen minutes with each child, getting him or her ready for bed. And Jo takes turns in bringing one with her when she goes shopping, and Jim will take one when he goes on longer trips.

The Seeleys understand the importance of time alone for themselves too. The two of them reserve one night a week as "date night." At least once a year they also take a three-day weekend out of town away from the children.

Lord Jesus, Fill the Gap

Lord Jesus, fill the gap
between the love
I have given my children
and the love
they need.

RUTH STAPLETON

We need *love* in good measure, and we need to give it. We need to feel that we are *wanted and belong.* We need to feel that we are capable of *adequate achievement* so that we can manage to meet life's demands. We need *recognition* for what we achieve. We need to know *that the pleasure which our senses and our body can bring us* is permissible and good and that our enjoyment does not make us "bad." We need to feel *accepted and understood.* And finally we need to *feel worth while and essentially worthy in being uniquely the self that we are.*

DOROTHY W. BARUCH

Letting the child set the pace of intimacy—being there when they are needed and not pushing when they are not needed—this is the parents' job.

CLINEBELL AND CLINEBELL

In their book *Intimate Marriage*, Clinebell and Clinebell define what parent-child intimacy is not. It is not:

1. Making the child a substitute spouse. Parents must lean on each other, not on their children.
2. Living out the parents' unfulfilled lives through their children.
3. "Sacrifice." What a father gives of *himself* to his child is more important than what he provides for them financially. (Adequate economic support *is* a form of self-giving, of course.)
4. Peership. Parents need to be in charge. The opposite is the authoritarian relationship which does not allow the child to ask questions or express negative feelings.

With your husband:
  learn to share responsibilities
  keep working at a deeper, happier marriage relationship
  tell your mate how you feel
  study together a few books on child development
  plan family outings.

I believe in [sexual] equality, but at the same time . . . the man should be the head of the family, for the sake of family unity. I don't like . . . neglecting the main things for a woman, which are the children, the husband. [In Egypt] We don't want to make it such a confrontation. I need my husband and he needs me. Equality in salaries, in jobs, this is what I want. But if the relationship between the husband and wife is good, he will not sit there and tell the wife to do everything. He will help.

JIHAN SADAT

How to Develop Good Relationships With Adolescent Children

It needs courage to let our children go, but we are
trustees and stewards and have to hand them back to
life—to God. As the old saying puts it: "What I gave
I have." We have to love them and lose them.

ALFRED TORRIE

"Why do you still set a time for me to be in at night? Don't
you trust me?" Nineteen-year-old Beth stood facing her mother,
fingering her keys, dark eyes flashing. Beth's reaction, typical of
many emerging into young adulthood, voiced the need for her
parents to establish a new relationship with her.

Parents sometimes procrastinate in switching from control-
ling to supportive roles for a number of reasons, some conscious, some unconscious. Some fear it is an admission that
they, the parents, are getting old. Becky, in a college class I
attended, told of how her father's company always gave a
Christmas dinner party for the families of the executives. Becky
is older than her brother and sister by eight and ten years.

"The little kids were always allowed to go to the dinner,"
Becky said, "but I had to stay home. This year I insisted I go.
Dad's colleagues expressed surprise when they met me. Their
wives said to Mother, 'We didn't know you had a daughter this
age!' Mother was furious, because she had to face up to her
age."

Some parents fear losing the attention, affection, and assis-
tance of their children.

"What can I do with my mother-in-law?" one young bride
asked. "She calls every day. Her husband is often out of town
on business, and she expects Dick, who is my husband and her
son, to come over and repair every leaky faucet or clogged drain

72

or just to come and talk to her—or rather, listen to her talk. I've been thinking we should move just far enough away so a telephone call would be a toll call."

Unconsciously, perhaps, this mother felt she should be rewarded by her son for her efforts when he was a child. When he was little, she had allowed him to absorb most of her time and money. Now she feared losing his attention and affection.

Not so Mrs. Cruse Blackburn of Southern California. Blind since she was three years old, she had been dependent on her son, Raymond, since her husband died in 1971. But when Raymond wanted to marry, Cruse gladly released him. "God will have some way of looking after me," she said cheerfully.

Some parents fear that the children, lacking good judgment, will make mistakes. Strange, isn't it, how we forget that one of the ways we learn is by making mistakes. Consider the attitude of the father in the story of the Prodigal Son in Luke 15. Surely his wise father-mind told him his son's request was foolish. But the father knew his son would have to learn some lessons on his own, and so he not only let his son go, but gave him his inheritance.

We forget also that God has given to each of us the right to make mistakes. A father who had suffered heartache from the waywardness of two of his children wrote:

> Parents need to learn that there comes a time in the life of every person when he has a "right to be wrong." Development into maturity and independence involves decision making, and always carries with it the potential of error, whether deliberate or not. Thus to be human is to have the right to be wrong. This "right" does not make a wrong decision right; neither does it absolve from the consequences of wrong choices. But our children have the "right to be right" and the "right to be wrong."

Sometimes the child is the one who is reluctant to break away from his parents. Then the parents must gently push him from the nest.

Sharon was only nineteen when she wanted to get married. Her parents warned her that there would be problems because her fiancé, Steve, came from an entirely different background. Sharon didn't think so. Three months after their marriage, Sharon showed up at home with complaints against Steve.

"We think Steve is a fine young man, and evidently you do too, or you wouldn't have married him," her parents said and sent her back to Steve. And thus they nudged her from the nest when she wanted to crawl back in.

What then can we do to help our young people achieve liberation from complete dependence on us and develop into responsible adults?

Constantly encourage them to become independent. Parents vary in the way in which they grant freedom to their children. Some are lenient when the children are young and then restrict and prohibit more and more as they get older. Others maintain the same rules throughout childhood, adolescence, and even on into adulthood. Still others apply the most restraints when the child is young and then little by little allow more and more freedom.

When the first method is followed, when a child is clamped down on more and more as he gets older and older, he is apt to erupt like a volcano. On the other hand, if the parents do not release their hold gradually, the child will feel insecure when pushed from the nest. "My parents did everything for me until I graduated from high school. Then suddenly they told me I was on my own," one girl confided. "I was petrified. For weeks I couldn't sleep."

"I know," another one said, "only it happened to me when I was twenty. 'You're an adult now,' my parents said. Did they expect me suddenly to change overnight? If they had let me make decisions little by little and had reassured me of their help if I needed it, I would have felt much more secure."

Encouraging our eaglets to fly is a process usually requiring two decades or more in time and much love, sacrifice, patience, and understanding. When freedom is granted according to the responsibility shown, the child grows and develops into an independent young person.

Actually the parent knows we never really are independent, but rather interdependent. He knows his child will realize this too as he matures. But the road to learning the necessity and value of interdependence is often over the bumpy, uncomfortable road of independence. Consequently, to rear a child so he becomes self-reliant and independent of his parents is one of the primary and most important tasks of a parent.

Be patient and accepting even when you can't understand or agree with their behavior. They might not be as demonstrative with their love and affection as they were formerly. "Don't kiss me!" we'll hear, maybe even, "Don't touch me!" Their remarks might make us feel as though we have leprosy; but we shall have to remind ourselves that when our children utter these stay-away warnings, it isn't because they love us less, but because they are trying to break their dependence on us. It may hurt when we see them pouring out their affection on their friends and possibly even on some older friends whom they have chosen to be their confidants. We may be tempted to feel slighted, unloved, unappreciated, but we need to withstand the temptation to indulge in tears, complaining, or self-pity of any kind. Nor should we insist they show us affection, but instead rejoice that our children truly are maturing.

Our growing children might not confide in us as much anymore. "Don't ask me!" "Forget it!" "You wouldn't understand!" "Leave me alone, won't you?" Over and over we may hear this. We need to respect this desire on their part for privacy and their desire to work things out on their own.

One mother noticed that her adolescent daughter would begin to share and then abruptly stop. Finally she asked her daughter why she stopped. "Oh," said the girl, shrugging, "it sounds silly when I say it. You wouldn't understand."

In her teens this sensitive woman had been bereaved of her mother. With no one to confide in she had poured out her woes into her diary. She had kept her diary. She dug it out now. "Maybe this would interest you," she said casually to her daughter. After that Mother became a more frequent confidante.

But if the young adult chooses not to confide, his father and mother do well not to question, probe, or demand they be told everything.

Young adults might exaggerate. Before you get furious about something they have said, go into your room and rock for a while in your rocking chair. Ask yourself if they have exaggerated for effect's sake. A friend of mine told of overhearing a telephone conversation of her daughter.

"Oh, your mom got all upset, did she?" Silence. "That's too bad." Silence. "My mom? My mom knows I mean only a fourth of what I say."

Well, thought that mother, *I hadn't known that before, but I'm sure glad to learn it now.*

Their grooming habits might irritate us. When young people choose to dress and groom themselves in a different fashion, parents protest, explode, ridicule, demand reformation, suffer in martyrlike silence, ignore not only the style of dress but also the young person himself, resign themselves to it, or strike a compromise—some even adopt the fashions themselves. Perhaps the happiest route lies in recognizing that both parents and children have rights.

After a year away from home, Tom moved back to attend a community college. "His casual dress was hard for us to accept," his mother confessed. "His long, unkempt hair particularly annoyed my husband. Finally my husband said, 'Look, son, I can stand to sit and look across the table at long hair, but I can't stand it when it's uncombed. Either comb it or eat your meals on a tray in your room.' Tom sputtered and then began to comb his hair."

Our children might not adopt our values. "What do you do," a tall, graying, highly intelligent man asked, "if your children scorn and ridicule what you hold dear?" He was touching on what can be a very sore point, especially for fathers.

The wrong reaction, of course, is to despair. True, when a father cannot look at his children and see in them that which satisfies him, and when he feels completely helpless and frustrated in doing anything about this, he is tempted to despair. He may mask his despair with disgust—or a thousand little disgusts—expressed towards the child. The child, it seems, can do nothing to please him. Or the father may revert to sulking and acting like a selfish child himself. Or he may identify with his child, against his own convictions, adopting his child's standards and philosophy as his own, when in reality they are not. But when a middle-aged person reverts to adolescent behavior or thought, it wreaks havoc with his integrity.

But what can a parent do?

In the first place, we need to reexamine what we claim to be our set of values and the actual way in which we live our lives. We cannot hold double standards. As our children observe day by day how we live and talk and act, they will pick up the values we model. We cannot say to our child, "Don't drink; don't smoke," if we drink and smoke. If we want them to show appreciation and gratitude, we need to ask ourselves, "Do they see me expressing appreciation?" If we want them to be free of the lust for money and material things, we shall have to examine ourselves as to how much desire for these actually does control *our* lives. *Why* are we working? So, in some cases, if we see our children adopting values with which we are not happy, we may have to say, "We're going to stop some of the crazy things we've been doing." And in some cases, if they adopt values different from ours we may have to be humble enough to ask, "Are they choosing more wisely than we are?"

Maintain an attitude of love and trust rather than one of guilt. Many parents suffer guilt because they wonder if they raised their children in the right way.

"We had five children," one woman said, "and they were just far enough apart in years so all five have been brought up in a different way, depending on which method of child rearing was in vogue when the child was born. Goodness knows which method was best, or if any of them were any good."

There's little point in fretting about the past. If you did your best, leave it in God's hands. He has a way of compensating for our mistakes.

But what do you do when you *know* you've made mistakes in raising your children? "I came to know Christ only a couple of years ago," one mother said. "If I had known him earlier, I would have taught my children altogether different values." The answer is: Live Christ now. Your children will see the difference He has made in you.

"I've been a Christian all our married life," another mother said, "but that doesn't mean I've done everything right. I sometimes became very irritated, and even angry, with my children. Sometimes I punished them unjustly. When I think of it, I feel so guilty."

How good it is to know that not only does God forgive us, but He also enables our children to recover from injury and to make adjustments. As Reuel Howe expresses in his book *Creative Years:* "The mistakes we make are not nearly as powerful as the love we give." Friends of ours have seen this truth beautifully portrayed. They adopted a two-year-old boy who had been severely mistreated as a baby. Wounded and hurt, he would lash out at them. He attacked other children and was very hyperactive. Sometimes his hostile and contentious behavior caused his mother's patience to run thin. Then she would punish him in anger. Minutes later, in remorse, she would weep. But always she loved the child passionately, and she would ask his forgiveness when she had done wrong. Today that child, of all their children, brings them the most joy. The old wounds are healed, and he is deeply grateful to his parents for their love.

Many parents today are struggling with guilt feelings as their children live together with others without getting married or have babies out of wedlock or divorce after only a few years of married life. "What did we do wrong?" they cry.

Maybe nothing. We need to remember that though we can influence and guide, the final choice rests with the child. As we said before, we have to give our children the same right God gives us, the right to choose. And we need to remember too the strong outside forces exerted on our children. Some experts have said that the peer influence on youth is as great, or almost as great, as the home influence.

But if we are not to feel guilty, what should be our response to a child who has deeply hurt us? The father of two wayward children referred to earlier says:

The Christian parent will continue to hold on to his child, come what may, with the bonds of faithful love. Parents can perhaps, if they wish, permit the hard experience of life to "kill" their love for a child who has spitefully used them. But, conversely, they can, if they will, continue to love that wayward individual in the hope (maybe it will prove vain) that he will someday respond and that someday reconciliation will occur.

A parent with a Christian perspective knows something about the unselfishness of the love of God for His wayward children. Such was the love which prompted Him to send to earth His Redeemer-Son and which moves His Spirit to work continuingly in His erring children for their forgiveness and spiritual growth. This is the kind of love which Christians are exhorted to reveal in their dealings with other people—pure, unselfish love, never achieved by humans but always worth the effort. The forgiven—unto seventy times seven—are in turn forgivers unto seventy times seven.

One mother shared:

Joan came home five months pregnant. She wanted to keep her baby, but neither she nor the boy who was the baby's father wanted to marry. What were we to do? The baby was born, a beautiful, healthy child. Now Joan wants to go back to college and make something of her life. I'm caring for the baby. Of course, I wish circumstances had been different, but I'm rather enjoying having a baby to care for again. And Joan loves her baby dearly, because she feels God used the whole circumstance to help her get right with Him and get her values straightened out.

Another mother, herself a widow, confessed:

I was heartbroken when Annie told me she was pregnant, but how could I turn Annie out on the

street? A short while later I came down with an illness
that kept me in bed for many months. How grateful I
was for Annie's loving care for me. The baby was born.
I went back to work when I recovered. What a treat it
was to come home every evening to a sparkling house,
a hot dinner, laundry done, and a cooing grandson!
Now that he is older we have him in a Christian nur-
sery, and Annie is back at college. We're believing
roses will bloom out of the ashes.

When a divorced daughter or son comes home with small
children and all the attendant problems, parents find themselves really cast on God to understand what is the Christian
way to respond. They forgive, love, and accept, yes—but does
their responsibility end with this, or are they expected to raise
another family just when they were looking forward to years of
more freedom? How good that God has promised us wisdom,
each of us in our individual, differing situations.

Another heartbreaking situation arises when children leave
or run away from home and never contact their parents. Then to
hang on in love and trust is an acid test. The parents will be
tempted to think the child cherishes no love or gratitude toward
them at all. At times like this we need to cling to the fact that it
is almost impossible to kill a child's love for his parents.

"It's an odd psychological fact," a counselor at a home for
juvenile-delinquent boys told me, "but boys who have nothing
to go back to at all get really homesick and want to return
home."

Now if this is true for children who have been mistreated,
how much stronger must be the love ties where the home atmosphere has been warm and accepting. So form a mental image of
the kind of person you want your son or daughter to become
(hopefully, you will let God direct your desires). Focus on that
image. Thank God it will be so. And then begin to treat your
young person as the responsible individual you believe he will
become.

Above all, don't let relationships rupture. Emily, a
mother of several young-adult children related: Vir-

ginia was dating a divorced man considerably older than her. He had custody of the two children from his previous marriage. Other factors also caused us concern. Their racial and cultural backgrounds were very different. We talked and talked with Virginia. It got us no place. So we prayed that God would stop the marriage. But though I prayed and prayed, I could get no assurance that God would answer my prayer. My frustration mounted.

The relationship with our daughter worsened to the point where Virginia moved out. I continued to pray. Finally it occurred to me that I should change my prayer. I began to pray that the good relationship we had had with Virginia before would be restored. Immediately I was assured I was praying for the right thing. My attitude changed, and Virginia's also did. We were reconciled. In the end she did marry, and the marriage is a happy one. Her husband has become a dedicated Christian, and our relationships have never been better.

Walls often come between parents and children when the young people go away to college, especially if neither parents nor children write or call.

"Our son never writes," a troubled mother told me. "He used to call collect. Last time he did, his father asked him why he didn't write. Joe said there wasn't anything that would interest us. That really made my husband blow up. He told me not to accept any more pay calls from him."

"And what did you do?"

Her eyes dropped to the floor. "I stopped writing too."

"But you're unhappy about it?"

"Of course. He's coming home in a couple of weeks' time for Christmas, and his father is ready to blister him."

Here is a situation where the parents can determine the future of their relationship with their child. Being a parent calls for infinite patience. Sometimes we need to go not only the second mile but the third and fourth too. A guiding question to ask ourselves is: What can we do to make the relationship between our child and us the best one it can possibly be? If we keep in view our ultimate goal, a continuing good relationship with our child who has become independent from us, it will help us see present difficulties in perspective, and we shall discover we can afford to be generous and forgiving. Time matures all of us. With maturity comes a different point of view. Sometimes it takes longer for some to mature than others. Then we have to wait and show *our* maturity.

The father of an able young doctor tells how when his son left for college, he tossed him a couple of quarters. "If you need me, call," he said. Years later, the night of the boy's wedding, as the son was saying good-bye to his father, he tossed his dad two quarters. The father fingered them, then, with a smile tossed them back. A few weeks later the son bumped into a problem and called his father. "That would never have happened," the father said, "if the quarters hadn't kept the way open all the previous years."

It will be worth every effort to maintain good relationships with our children. In the years ahead we shall need them, and they will need us.

Be thankful for the help others give. We are not alone. Good teachers play an important role. A trusted pastor can become a true friend. Or our young-adult children may seek out other older adults in whom they feel free to confide. Don't be jealous of these relationships. Welcome them. Encourage them. Others can make our job easier.

Remember that in the end your children are God's. Have we given them to Him? Then we can trust Him and never give up hope.

Appreciate your children. Delight in the joy, freshness, and vigor they bring to a home. Accept the help their strong, young arms and untiring bodies can give. Enjoy their skills and abilities manifested in song and music, in arts and crafts, in baking, cooking, and sewing, in carpentry and painting. Encourage their keen discernment, their glowing idealism. Rejoice in their warm love for Jesus, for kindnesses they show others, for their compassion. They will surprise you with their knowledgeable conversation, spiked with humor and colorful language, seasoned with a reflective thought you wouldn't have guessed them capable of yet. Value the loyal, clear-eyed friendship they offer you. Appreciate them when they correct you or point out your inconsistencies. Respect them for being themselves, unique, marvelous individuals. Consider these qualities, and in your bedroom at night, as you and your mate share the joy they have brought you that day, smile in the dark and say, "How could we ever have brought such lovely persons into being?"

As your heart is warmed, you will discover a wonderful miracle taking place. *You* are being appreciated.

If we genuinely appreciate our young people and express our appreciation, a bonus for them will be the flowering of self-confidence. They will need self-confidence. They will need to be assured they are of value, that they can find their places in society and become contributing members, that they can control the controllable factors in life. They will need this if they are going to take wings and fly, to swoop and soar and rise above the problems and pettiness of our troubled old world.

By becoming helpers and guides, acknowledging our common humanity and weaknesses, mutually turning to God, from whom all love and faith comes, we as parents can work thus for good relationships that will encourage our eaglets to fly.

As mother [the shalom woman] looks for father to be truly father, a partner in the entire parenting process. Although "mom" has been excoriated and the finger of society pointed to her as responsible for all juvenile problems, the role of the father cannot be minimized in its influence upon children. Cruel, domineering, neglectful absentee fathers must share responsibility for actions as they affect their offspring. Most middle-class fathers will disclaim being any of the above; but if they are totally involved with a life away from home, they will surely have a negative influence in the life of their children.

MARGARET WOLD

I have never yet heard any middle-aged man or woman who worked with his or her brains express any regret for the passing of youth.

DOROTHY SAYERS

Though our mouths were full of song as the sea,
Our tongues of exultation as the fulness of its waves,
And our lips of praise as the plains of the firmament:
Though our eyes gave light as the sun and moon;
Though our hands were outspread as the eagles of heaven,
And our feet were swift as hinds,
Yet should we be unable to thank Thee,
O Lord, our God and God of our parents,
And to bless Thy name for even one of the countless thousands
And tens of thousands
Of kindnesses which thou hast done by our parents and by us.

JEWISH PRAYER

Mother to Over 350 Children

Love feels no burden, thinks nothing of trouble, attempts what is above its strength, pleads no excuse of impossibility; for it thinks all things possible. He who does not love would faint and lie down.

THOMAS À KEMPIS

Mrs. Geraldine Lewis of Long Beach mothered 350 children before she was thirty years of age. She did it as a participant in the Good Neighbor Program of Los Angeles County which places children caught in crisis situations, temporarily separated from their parents, in foster homes.

"When I was approached about becoming a short-term foster parent, at first I said *no*," Geraldine said. Slender and supple, she curled up on the big, plastic-upholstered davenport in their living room and began to talk rapidly and in a low voice.

"Then I said, *yes*, I would be a foster parent, but no teenagers. The first one brought to me was a seventeen-year-old who came from a wealthy home in Palos Verdes and whose parents were alcoholics."

A long succession followed that troubled teenager: three sets of twins, about thirty teenagers, but most of the children have been under twelve years of age. They came dirty, with matted hair, some with lice, babies with diaper rash from waist to knees. Teenagers were high on drugs. Geraldine nursed one infant through withdrawal symptoms from heroin. One summer was a nightmare: two and one-half months of consecutive cases of chicken pox.

"The hardest is to love a child and then let him go," she confessed. "Without the Lord, I couldn't do it. But there are rewards, too. Like the teenager picked up on the beaches at

Venice. She was married to a Hell's Angel at fifteen. She was brought to me, unwashed, unkempt—a mess! The next day we went to her 'home' to get her remnants of clothes—and what an unbelievable filthy place it was!''

Gerry shut her eyes as she remembered. "She had been in school only six weeks during the last three years. 'My mother told me, but never *made* me do anything,' she said. We enrolled her in school. She graduated with *A's* and *B's*. One Thanksgiving morning she knelt here at the davenport and gave her heart to Christ. Her first marriage was annulled. She married a fine Christian boy. The day of her wedding I wore a lovely orchid corsage—her gift to me.

"My husband gave away another of our girls. Many of them come back and help me with the children I have in my care. One summer we became 'grandparents' twice in a week. One of our girls, who was in a detention hall, we brought back for a weekend visit once a month. We receive cards and letters. One Indian girl, who had been on mescaline, couldn't bring herself to say, 'I love you,' or 'I care for you.' But sitting on her bed one night, she said, 'Do you know how many people are going to be at your funeral?' And once the supervisors of Los Angeles County called me before a group of 1,500 people and presented me with a huge award."

Geraldine's church supported her. Ladies baby-sat, provided transportation to doctors, collected good clothes, and sewed.

"Surely one of the most rewarding aspects is what it has meant for my own spiritual life," Gerry said. "I have learned I can turn to the Lord for anything—a dryer that breaks down, a child who is difficult to manage, strength for a new day when there has been little sleep the night before. Over and over I have proven God's faithfulness."

She chuckled. "There have been humorous touches too. I have a stroller into which I can tuck four children. One day a lady stopped me and said, 'Honey, I've just gotta ask you. I never see you pregnant, and yet you keep showing up with new babies.' And a police officer eyed me one day and said, 'Ma'am, you must either be a devout Catholic or a sexy Protestant!' ''

The two Lewis children, Pamela and Charles, benefited from

their mother's reaching out. "It taught them tolerance, patience, and an appreciation of how good they have it," Mrs. Lewis said. "I have seen them, too—always seeking out the underdog themselves, even at school."

And then Gerry closed as she had begun, "But without the Lord, we couldn't have done it."

The Heart of the Childless
Is Gladdened With Children

Simply having children does not necessarily make a woman a mother, nor does not having children make a woman not a mother.

The world was passing Marion Gould by. Severe acne masked the attractiveness of her bright, pleasant face and isolated her from friends and fun. Marion watched friends date and become engaged and listened to their plans for marriage.

Never mind, Marion thought. *I'll be a career woman.* Both the education and medical fields appealed to her. She was a brilliant student and won a scholarship to a college in her hometown. But these were the Depression years, and Marion's parents just didn't have the money needed for Marion to attend college.

"Never mind," Marion comforted her father. "You have given me a prize far greater than any education in helping me to know God."

"He'll never let you down either," her father said. "Only," he paused, considering her education, "I wish it could have been different." He thought for a while, then added, "Why don't we pray that you will find work? Then you can save your money and go to college."

But it was not to be. Marion's father became ill. Cancer, the doctors said—terminal. After two pain-filled years, he died, leaving Marion with staggering medical bills to pay and an ailing mother to care for.

Marion enjoyed the work she was doing in an office, but she kept praying: "Lord, surely there must be more to life than just earning a living. Surely you must have some plan for me, something that will have purpose and meaning."

A door opened. Her pastor wished the children of their church could worship on a level that would be more meaningful to them. Would Marion be willing to assume responsibility for a Children's Church on Sunday mornings? "Yes," Marion said.

"It called for a lot of imagination and hard work," Marion admitted. "There were no set programs or lesson plans, but I saw it as a wonderful opportunity to get close to the children, win them to Christ, and lead them into fields of service for Him."

Marion understood that "getting close" meant playing with the children, too, so she planned picnics, Halloween parties, Christmas parties, outings. Every Sunday morning she arose early to pick up underprivileged children who had no other way of getting to church.

God touched the hearts of the children. They began to respond. The work was rewarding, but still Marion was not satisfied. "You must have something else for me to do, Lord," she prayed. "I can do more. Besides, I should be pointing the children to interests beyond themselves."

A friend suggested she investigate the work of the American Council of the Ramabai Mission, in India. Marion sat down to write a letter.

At the same time, at the mission in India, two little Brahmin girls arrived. Their parents had died. The little girls were considered witches and had been cast out. A former orphan of the Ramabai Mission found the starving, frightened children and brought them to the Mission. Sherada (*wisdom*) was six, Seroj (*lotus*) was four.

When Miss Patterson received Marion's letter of inquiry she wrote, asking if Marion would like to support Seroj. Thus began a mother-daughter relationship that was to continue for more than twenty years.

Marion not only sent monthly support for Seroj, but loved her as her own. Christmas, birthdays, special days were remembered with gifts. Weekly letters were sent. In time Seroj could write English and answer Marion's letters directly.

And always Marion prayed for Seroj.

She began to see her prayers answered. When Seroj was in fifth grade, she said she believed in Jesus and wanted to be baptized. When she graduated from high school, she said she wanted to train for service. Nursing was open, so she enrolled.

A number of young men approached Seroj, but her heart was set on a young doctor who showed her attention and affection. But Seroj had misinterpreted his attentions. When he made it clear he was not thinking of marriage there were tears, heartache, and disappointment for Seroj.

"I wrote her," Marion said, "counseling her to seek God's will and reminding her that God loved her."

As Seroj began to pray, a Christian family in another part of India was also seeking God's guidance in regard to the right girl for their youngest son to marry. They had a list of thirty-seven names. As they prayed, they felt they wanted to learn more about Seroj. So the young man and his older brother traveled to Mukti where Seroj was to meet them.

"It was love at first sight!" Seroj wrote excitedly to Marion. "We talked and talked. Suresh explained how he was studying in America to become a pastor. My heart leaped with joy and praise to God!"

So it was that after twenty years Marion met the daughter she had loved and prayed for. A year later Marion became a grandmother when a little boy was born to Seroj and Suresh Borde. And then Marion waved them off as they flew back to India. Suresh serves now as the only evangelist in Aurangabad, a city of over 165,253 with twenty-four colleges and great opportunities to work among young people.

In the meantime, during the years Seroj was in high school, Marion had told an American missionary in Korea about the work of the Ramabai Mission. Her friend had been able to incorporate some of the procedures and policies of the older, experienced Ramabai Mission in the Compassion Orphanage which he was founding. He was grateful to Marion for her help.

Seroj was launched in life. The Compassion Orphanage in Korea was engaged in a ministry of caring. The objective Marion had set for herself in the Children's Church was being realized; over 200 children had committed themselves to Christ. Her position as one of the secretaries to a president of a large corporation in St. Paul, Minnesota, was challenging and satisfying. Her salary was enough to share with children of nieces and nephews and to help support many, many missionaries. And still Marion was not satisfied.

So she adopted Yung Ae (which means *lovely child*), a homeless waif of the Korean War, about whom no one knew anything, and began to love and support and pray for her as she had for Seroj. Today Yung Ae is attending a trade school where she is learning to make clothing.

Retirement was drawing closer for Marion. "But surely, Lord," she prayed, "there is yet one other I can love for you." And so she accepted Saraswati, a twelve-year-old Indian girl whose mother had lived with a man in common-law marriage. When both parents died, Saraswati was left to care for her eight-year-old brother and six-year-old sister. They were starving when they were brought to the mission.

Today, Marion, a poised, radiant, attractive lady, is vibrantly alive. She leaves one with the impression of a person deeply fulfilled. Marion herself says simply, "My life could have been a barren and defeated one, but what glorious joy there has been for me in experiencing the fulfillment of God's purposes. 'Oh, the depth of the riches of the wisdom and knowledge of God! How unsearchable are His judgments and His ways past finding out!' "

Homage to Ma Miller

There is no surpirse more magical than the surprise of being loved. It is the finger of God on a man's shoulder.

CHARLES MORGAN

Often I have been haunted by the irrepressible anxiety: if Ma Miller had not guided my hand with her own in trying to write the alphabet, what would have become of my life today? There are many possibilities.

I would have been one of the restless multitudes of natives roving the forests, wading through swamps, digging the earth to eke out a living . . . I would have become a porter, a laborer of some sort, one of the thousand and one jobs uneducated native men in Africa do. There is nothing bad, of course, in living a simple life. But what I would have missed (which I consider extremely valuable) is the ability to write. Writing can be a confession, a search for salvation, and it can make life interesting, coherent, worthwhile. This I would have missed if it had not been for Ma Miller.

My father had the fancy when I was four or five that I must know book. All of us in the family began looking at my future in a romantic way: I would know how to put my thought on white paper and send it far away to someone else, and I could talk to him while absent physically. I would get a lot of money, go to the white man's country, ride an airplane, etc., most important of all take my people out of poverty and oppression. These, I think, chiefly comprised the motivation which led my father to take me to the Kpolopele Lutheran Mission.

When we entered the mission I discovered a new world,

self-contained, entirely different from the world I knew. The lawn was cut low and well trimmed, the eaves of thatch roofs were also trimmed neatly. An atmosphere of health, beauty, and order pervaded everything. Perhaps all the students were in school.

A distant relative of mine, Thomas, took us to Ma Miller's office. She lived in a square house with plastered mud walls and thatch roof. My father and I sat on a bamboo bench covered with a colorful sheet of home-spun fabrics. My brother-in-law and Thomas sat opposite to us. It was a moment of tension, but my eyes could not be restrained from gliding over the beautiful pictures hanging on the walls, pretty flowers in glass jars, carefully packed books and colored papers lying on shelves. Ma Miller was typing very fast, stopping sporadically to scribble something on a piece of paper. It was one trait of Ma Miller's which I admired through the years—her ability to think very fast and accurate and work without respite.

She looked lively. Her face, with gold-rimmed glasses, had an austere, penetrating look, and her grizzled hair was tied in a beautiful knot at the back of her head. She was beautiful. When Thomas began speaking she turned towards us with a serious face.

She looked me over briefly and said something to Thomas (he was the only one who understood English). "The white woman said you may come to Gargbelei to school each afternoon," Thomas said to me.

I found I could read quite well, but my special problem was in learning to write the alphabet. The teacher usually wrote a simple sentence (e.g. I see father) on the top of the wooden slates, painted black, which we used. And then with a white chalk we tried to write the same sentence several times, imitating his handwriting.

The letter which proved difficult for me to write was "S." I had the mind of the perfectionist which compelled me to master this letter before proceeding to another one. I fought frantically with myself to master it, but each attempt seemed to put me away from achieving my goal.

The teacher grew impatient, grew extremely reprimanding.

He began giving very little attention to me when almost half a year could not get me over this block.

I remember Father coming to the classroom one afternoon to see my progress. He watched me sitting on the mat, the slate laying on my stretched lap, trying furtively to write. The teacher watched me, shook his head and then said with resignation that I was not able to learn anything. The white woman would come the next day and would decide if I could go on with school. It was clear to Father and me that I would not redeem the hope and promise he had invested in me. The future loomed with terror, with the feeling of inadequacy and darkness.

When Ma Miller stepped into the classroom the next afternoon her face beamed with a broad smile. She observed each student and the work he was doing.

I was all tensed up, my hand trembling, praying that she would pass me by in the same way the angel of death passed by the houses of Israel's sons.

She nodded approval of the work of many of the students. At last she came to me. I felt her uncomfortable presence over me, and I expected something terrible to happen. My heart bounced against my ribs violently, and in my eyes the evening sun turned feverish and ominous.

After I went through a few moments of torturing effort with the chalk and the slate, she bent down, held my hand, tucked with the chalk, and guided it across the slate until I wrote correctly my first English word, "See."

My education began at that moment. At least the path I wanted to travel became clear and open.

Each one has a memory of an encounter, whether with God or man, that may mean a great deal to him, that may help significantly to shape his future, an encounter that is never to be forgotten. Having Ma Miller guide my hand to form a beautiful "S" was such an encounter for me.

I owe her so much. I love her so much. It cannot be said how hard it will be to bear the farewell when she says goodbye to Africa and leaves us.

WILTON SANKAWULA

Korean Child

Be still, my soul: the Lord is on thy side;
Bear patiently the cross of grief or pain;
Leave to thy God to order and provide;
In every change he faithful will remain.

KATHERINE VON SCHLEGEL

I was born in Seoul, Korea, on June 10, 1958—I think! No one is absolutely sure of the date or place, because I was either found and brought to the orphanage or my mother left me there. I guess I'll never know my real parents and the situation.

About this time in the United States in Oceanside, California, a couple had heard about the many homeless Korean babies in this orphanage and, after much prayer and thought, decided to adopt twin girls. They named them Sheryl and Sharon. On the journey to the States, Sharon became ill and died. The couple was stricken and, after burying Sharon, went to their home with only one baby in their arms.

When the agency heard about Sharon's death, they wanted the couple to have another child, and I was the replacement. I was flown to the airport in Los Angeles, where my new father and mother greeted me and took me home to be with my new sister, Sheryl.

So at the age of seven months my life with this wonderful family began. My childhood was very happy, and my parents taught me many things by their example. My mother loved God, and the Holy Spirit filled her life with joy and peace. She was a beautiful, loving woman who cared about everyone. My dad was a quiet and loving man. He too was a Christian, but his manner was more subdued. He was understanding and patient.

I was proud to be a Korean-American. Whenever the kids

used to ask me why I had slanted eyes and my parents didn't, I'd stand up straight and tell them why—I was never ashamed to tell them all about it. It made me feel unique. As a little child, though, I never stopped to tell my parents how dearly I loved them. It was something I figured I'd say when I was grown up. Well, the opportunity never came for me to tell my mom.

Each year our family entered flower arrangements at the San Diego County Fair. On the way home from the fair in July, 1969, we had a tragic experience. A car sideswiped us. After what seemed an eternity, our car went out of control and collided with another car. My mom was killed instantly. My dad had to be taken to the hospital. My sister and I were not injured. The memory of it all is so fresh in my mind. That night after we came home from the hospital and tried to sleep we felt very alone and afraid. A wife and mother had been killed, and her husband and her two ten-year-old daughters would have to carry on now and somehow learn to live without her.

For the first time in our lives, Sheryl and I really began to know my dad. Our mother had taken care of us, but now it was Dad's turn. He was a reserved, sweet, and gentle man. He was wonderful to us, and we always tried to please him. We loved him very much and were very close to him. The three of us together learned to be more self-reliant and grew tremendously as individuals.

A few years later a youth team visited our church, and at that time I received the Lord Jesus as my Saviour. I had been brought up in a Christian home, but Jesus had no real meaning to me until I really committed my life to Him as my Lord. I was fourteen years old, and from that day on God's Holy Spirit taught me and helped me to grow; I think it was to prepare me for the road ahead.

In two years we were again to be filled with the sadness of losing a loved one. During June, 1974, my dad went to the hospital. In surgery they found a malignant, cancerous tumor. He knew his life would end; it was only a matter of time. On October 7, 1974, my father passed away, freed from the pain he had suffered those last few months. But I was able to thank him for all he had done for us and tell him how much I loved him.

Now both my mother and father had passed from this life to be with the Lord. And then through the blessing of God we were given a new set of parents—our third set! Before my father died, he appointed the pastor of our church and his wife to be legal guardians for my sister and me. What a gift of God this was! Not only could we have new parents, but they already were friends whom we dearly loved and respected. How wonderful that my sister and I could stay together to have a home and a family and, most of all, to feel God's presence and care through our loss, knowing He would care for us in the future also. Praise God!

I pray that through my story you may see God's steadfast love and care, and will be encouraged to use the strength and courage He has available for you to meet both life and death.

ELLI WIDEN

What the World Needs Today

The greatest need of the world today is the kind of person who can survive and thrive and make a creative contribution to his community.

The most-needed personality qualities today have certain built-in specifications that have emerged as essential by specialists in human development and societal well-being. Some of these qualities are:

1. Ability to love others, seen and unseen, as oneself;
2. Willingness to live with difference;
3. Inner peace that can wait for satisfaction;
4. Competence to make rational decisions, with increasing integrity;
5. Eagerness to assume real responsibility for oneself and others;

6. Flexibility to be truly creative in new situations;
7. Joy of relating closely to nature and its wonders;
8. Satisfaction of helping others find fulfillment of their potential;
9. Excitement of curiosity and continual development of one's interests; and
10. Reverence for life in all its forms and functions.

EVELYN MILLIS DUVALL

O Divine Spirit,
who in all the events of life art knocking at the door of my heart,
    help me to respond to Thee.
I would take the events of my life as good and perfect gifts from
    Thee.
I would receive even the sorrows of life as disguised gifts from
    Thee.
I would have my heart open at all times to receive;
    at morning, noon, and night,
    in spring and summer and winter.
Whether Thou comest to me in sunshine or in rain,
    I would take Thee into my heart joyfully.
Thou art Thyself more than sunshine;
Thou art Thyself compensation for the rain.
It is Thee, and not Thy gifts, I crave.
Knock, and I shall open unto Thee. Amen.

GEORGE MATHESON

May I seek to live this day
    quietly, easily,
leaning on Your mighty strength
    trustfully, restfully,

meeting others in the path
  peacefully, joyously,
waiting for Your will's unfolding
  patiently, serenely,
facing what tomorrow brings
  confidently, courageously.

AUTHOR UNKNOWN

When the Last Child Leaves Home

Some people always sigh in thanking God.
ELIZABETH BROWNING

All parents sooner or later come to the day when the last child walks out of the home, and the house is empty. Although a certain measure of relief and a gratifying sense of accomplishment might be part of the experience, the overwhelming feeling usually is one of great loss. We experienced that feeling of loss prematurely. When we were in Africa our children had to leave home at the age of six and go away to boarding school. Painful though the experience was, yet it opened up to us some guidelines for meeting this crisis experience in life courageously and appropriately. Let me tell you how it was for us when the last one left, and how we learned to live with it.

He was only six years, four months, and five days old. It was past his bedtime, and we both were tired. I was on my knees, trying to make up his lower bunk bed. He was standing nearby.

We had been on the bus all day, making the trip from home, on the lower slopes of Mount Kilimanjaro in northern Tanzania, to this school, snuggled into the curve of a hillside overlooking the vast Rift Valley in Kenya. Arising at 5:15 in the morning, we had dressed and prepared and eaten our breakfast by candlelight. Then, after an hour-long drive to Moshi, at the base of Kilimanjaro, we had met a big bus that carried us the 300 miles to the Kenya school.

The journey had been tiring, as are most trips in East Africa.

Added to this was the strain on our whole family these last days as we prepared the children to leave again for a three-month term at a school far from home. This was David's first time.

He looked around the room. There was not much to lift drooping spirits. Three bunk beds, some open shelves for clothes, and an old settee. That was all. There were curtains at the windows but no pictures on the wall. This dormitory bore faint resemblance to the cozy, bright, gay room he had left at home.

"Guess it'll be all right," he ventured, drawing a deep breath. "Especially after I get used to it." A rolled-up pair of socks came hurtling at him from across the room. He ducked and grinned. "It might even be fun."

In my heart I cheered him and was not a little comforted myself.

So many children who leave home to go away to boarding school are completely bewildered and confused at first. They experience homesickness, but cannot understand or identify the emotion.

Ten minutes later the storm broke. There was a sudden rush across the room. A little red head buried itself in my skirts, as David always does when he is hurt.

Usually a child cries just with nose and eyes and noise from his mouth. This was different. Deep, racking sobs caused his little chest to heave up and down. "Don't leave me; don't leave me!"

I gathered him in my arms and held him close. He snuggled as he had when he was much smaller. We sat quietly until the sobs subsided. The little wet nose was buried deep in my breast. Then I recalled something that had happened just a few months earlier.

David had appeared for breakfast but had eaten nothing. The same happened at lunch. When I asked if he felt all right, he had quietly said *yes*.

But by midafternoon hunger had gotten the best of him. He had come in and asked for a sandwich. As he was eating it, he had confided, "D'yah know why I wasn't going to eat?"

"No, why?"

"Well, last night when I crawled up into your lap you said, goodness, I was getting big."

"You are."

"But you said you wouldn't be able to hold me much longer." He had paused, his nose wrinkled up with embarrassment; he had laughed self-consciously, then added, "I want to stay little so I can sit on your lap."

I had laughed too. Now the memory of it caused me to struggle for self-control.

I was to spend the night as a houseguest in one of the faculty homes. So I tucked David in bed and left him crying into his pillow.

The next morning I reached his dorm just as the little boys, decked out in their stiff, new, khaki uniforms, were filing out the door to go down to the dining hall. There, sixth in line, was a little red-haired boy with very red, swollen eyes.

He didn't say a word in greeting when he saw me, but just grasped my hand very tightly. We started down the road together.

"I couldn't find my socks this morning," he complained, sniffling. Then, in an altogether different tone, "*Wow!* Look at that tree house over there!

"These uniforms are so stiff I had to work awfully hard to get all the buttons buttoned," he said after a little silence. Then, again, "*Wow!* There's another tree house!"

During the whole walk down to the dining hall his chatter alternated between wistful comments and real interest in what he saw around him. I chuckled.

After breakfast he cheerfully walked off to classes. When classes were dismissed early, he came bounding up the hill, bubbling over with, "School is fun!" He literally danced as he talked.

We walked back to his dormitory to unpack his trunk and put his clothes away. That task finished, we wended our way down the hill again for the noon meal. "What time is it?" he asked.

"Eleven-thirty," I answered, thinking, *Only an hour and a half before I leave.*

"Oh, then I have a long time to be with you," he said happily, tightening his grasp on my hand.

"There will be a basketball game this afternoon. Are you going?"

"Yup," he said cheerfully. "Could you stay?"

"Mr. Olson goes at one. I'll have to leave then, David."

Outside the mess hall after lunch I asked him, "Do you want to say good-bye here or come down to the car?"

"I'll come down to the car," he replied.

I kissed him good-bye at the car. He grinned and wiped off his kiss with the back of his hand, as he always does to tease me. Then he stood and bravely waved good-bye until we were out of sight. I learned later that after we had gone he turned and ran toward his dormitory, crying all the way.

So I went home: to empty beds, to clothes hanging in the closets, to rooms always in order, to the oppressive quietness of the house all day long. Mealtimes passed quickly. No little Mr. Laggard now, who must dawdle over his food because there's so much to share with Mom and Dad. The familiar evening routine of seeing a tired, dirty child bathed, read to, prayed with, and tucked in bed was broken. But there was help.

After church on Sunday the wife of one of our African teachers came to the house. She took my hand in her own two strong young black ones and began, "Mama, when I saw you in church I knew you were eating bitterness, because your David and all the other children have gone away to school."

I bit my lip and blinked.

"I just wanted you to know, Mama, that I care, and I wanted to say *pole*."

Now *pole* is a little gem in the Swahili language. Pronounced "Pole-eh," it says, *I feel with you.*

Suddenly I was ashamed.

That year—it was 1965—12,000 seventh- and eighth-grade African students on Kilimanjaro had taken qualifying tests for entrance to high school. Only 961 had been granted admission. There just weren't buildings or teachers to care for more.

Judith could have thought of this. But she showed only love and sympathy and support. Her attitude towards us and our blessings humbled me, and I quit crying.

A short time later another missionary mother, who also had sent four to school and had none left at home, told me how an African woman had helped her regain perspective.

On Dottie's way home from accompanying her children to school, she had stopped to visit missionary friends who were working with a tribe in a remote village. While she was there, an older African had come to the house. Dottie had chatted with her.

In answer to a question, Dottie explained, "No, I don't live here. I'll be going home in a few days. But my heart knows no contentment in going home this time, because I go home to an empty house, a house without children."

The old lady clicked her tongue in sympathy and began to rub Dottie's arm. "Did they *all* die?"

Dottie realized her mistake. "Oh, no!" she clarified. "They're not dead! They've just gone away to boarding school to study."

The old lady's relief was evident. *"Watarudi tu!"* she comforted Dottie, her wrinkled face breaking into a toothless smile. *But then they will return!*

I laughed. "Will they ever," I said to Dottie. "All of them."

"Whoosh!" Dottie demonstrated with a sweep of her arm. "In that door—through the living room—clatter, clatter up the stairs . . . ."

"Stop!" I begged. "I'll let you think about cleaning up the mud tracked in. I'm going home to get started with painting the children's rooms. It's a lot easier when they're not around, and they'll be home before we know it."

When missionary parents have been able to adjust successfully to the separation from their children, I think a few general observations can be made.

- They knew separation was coming and prepared themselves and their children for it.
- They worked extra hard at cultivating good and close parent-child relationships.
- The mothers cultivated interests outside the home even

> when the children were small, so the void was filled when the children left home.
> - Husband-wife relationships were strong and in a process of growth.
> - The family accepted separation as normal for a missionary family and as part of the cross for the Christian. One missionary's young daughter wrote a note to her parents the day she left for boarding school and tucked it under her mother's pillow. Her mother found it after she was gone. The note read: "Dear Mom and Dad, You know I don't want to go away to boarding school. I'd much rather stay at home, but I know I must leave, because I am a missionary child . . . and I'm proud to be a missionary child."
> - Parents and children kept in touch through letters.
> - They realized the separation was not forever and that there would be visits.

It is my fondest hope that my children can somehow discover the three dimensions of the meaningful life that were outlined by their father in one of his sermons: that they will be able to "discover themselves, to discover their neighbors, and to discover God." For the discovery of these dimensions will enable them to become whole, contributing members of the world family of man.

CORETTA SCOTT KING

Enable us, O Lord, to lift up our hearts unto Thee
and let Thy Holy Spirit help us to worship Thee in spirit and truth.
We come before Thee, we the continual dependants on Thy goodness.

It is Thou who didst first bring us into existence.

Thou didst support us during the helplessness of infancy,
   the childishness of our early years,
   and Thou didst bear with us during the levity of youth.

Thou hast carried us through the various periods of our lives
   and hast brought us through numerous vicissitudes and dangers.

We look to Thee as the Author and Giver of all our blessings.

We acknowledge Thy goodness and long-suffering shown us as
   you have borne with our provocations.

We desire that Thy love will be shed abroad in our hearts that
   they may be warmed with more fervent and continual
   gratitude to Thee.

WILLIAM WILBERFORCE

How Can I Teach My Children to Pray?

God has no grandchildren.

In 1962 Bishop Dibelius wrote about the lessons the confessing church of Germany learned in the thirties when the Nazis were seeking to root out Christianity. He said:

> We learned many things during the struggle of the confessing church. But the best of all was that in those days there arose among most of us a new impulse to prayer . . . . We realized that confirmation instruction would remain a spiritually empty activity unless we succeeded in training the confirmands to pray, to pray practical, and simple, and daily prayers. We drew up our prayer lists, and we tried to help one another to offer these intercessions aright.

The first and most important step in teaching children to pray is at the same time simple and difficult: Set the example. No amount of talk will accomplish anything if your children do not see that prayer is important enough for you to spend time doing it. On the other hand, if they see the difference prayer makes in you, you might not have to say much at all.

I think back to my own childhood. I had witnessed an older brother and sister faithfully observing a quiet time every evening before going to bed. I assumed that this was the thing everyone did when he became a "grown-up Christian." So, without anyone suggesting that I do it, I just naturally followed. Perhaps the fact that I saw reflected in my brother's and sister's lives qualities I admired contributed to my patterning my life after theirs.

As I seek to leave an example for my children to follow, circumstances help discipline me. In order to escape the worst congestion of Los Angeles' Santa Ana Freeway (someone has called it the world's longest parking lot!) my husband leaves the house early. Our alarm clock flashes us awake shortly before five. The first thing I do is make our bed, so I won't be tempted to crawl back in! Then, husband breakfasted and on his way, with the children still asleep, the house is quiet. I am alone.

In her "Paths to Prayer" Marta Berg best describes what that early morning hour has come to mean to me: "Out of my prayer time I carry into my day an amazing harvest—release and guidance, strength and inner quiet . . . it's the heartbeat of my day."

Let's never underestimate the power of habit either. Routines established when the children were very, very small and added to bit by bit have become an accepted part of living. It is done as naturally as getting dressed in the morning.

Most mothers do not find it difficult or strange to pray with their young children. In fact, there is something about becoming a parent that draws many people closer to God. I am sure countless parents pray for their unborn child, and then, at last, when they can cradle their wee one in their arms it seems very natural to let their hearts ascend to God in thanksgiving and prayer.

Later, leading the little one to assume the posture of prayer and haltingly to articulate the first words of prayer is sheer joy.

But after the child becomes ten or thereabouts and abandons his rote prayers of childhood, it sometimes becomes more difficult to maintain the habit of prayer. And this is just where it is so important to continue to build the bridge that will span childhood into the teen years. If you let the practice of prayer slide for a few years, hoping to pick it up and assume it later, you quite likely will find yourself meeting with stiffening and rebellion.

There are many excellent devotional books that will help you through this difficult time with suggestions for making family prayer time interesting. Use them.

You can do various things to stimulate and maintain interest in prayer. In addition to prayer for forgiveness and prayers of thanksgiving, try prayers of intercession. Children love to pray for others.

For a time we tacked on a bulletin board the pictures of relatives and friends that came with Christmas greetings. From time to time this board became our prayer roster. Or we put the Christmas greetings in a basket and every evening drew out a card each and remembered that person in prayer.

Every month our church sends out suggestions for prayer. We have used these. I am one of a sixty-six-member prayer circle. When we receive a prayer call, we have often remembered the prayer request together.

Sometimes we follow the finger method which William Barclay suggested in one of his books. The thumb, being the closest to our body, represents those closest and dearest to us. The second finger is the pointer, so we think of our teachers and pastors. The third finger is the longest, reminding us of the VIPs—the leaders of our nation and community. The fourth finger is the weakest, suggesting the sick, the infirm, the sorrowing. The little finger is the most insignificant. Perhaps it can stand for ourselves. Remembering these guidelines, we volunteer to pray for certain fingers.

One of our children wrote down special requests on cards. When a prayer was answered, she made a note of it with the date. If no answer came, she simply wrote, "God said *no*."

So we come to the teen years and the need to teach our children—in one sense—to break away, to stand alone. For passing into adult Christian living requires more than participation in group worship, although this should continue.

Our pastor encouraged the young people in his instruction class to observe the daily quiet time. To help them he had them hand in a little written report every week. We were grateful for his support and help.

As our children approached the teen years we worked at

forming new habit patterns together. The first year I awakened them early. We gathered in the living room. After reading and discussing a few verses, together we considered prayer concerns. Reaching out beyond ourselves, we tried to remember definite community needs, the leaders of our land, the work of our church overseas, yes, even the staggering problems our nation faces.

The next year we tried to continue the same pattern but on an individual basis. As circumstances helped discipline me, so I tried to help my children also. I felt my responsibilities towards them were to awaken them early, to see that Bibles and devotional books were at hand and did not have to be hunted for, to see that they had privacy, to encourage—not nag—them.

On days when they were tired and it was hard to discipline oneself, I met briefly with them. Sometimes we read just one verse. Once in a while I read to them as they ate breakfast. Occasionally we stopped in the doorway and prayed together. Sometimes, when illness has hit the family hard, there were lapses. Sometimes we were just plain lazy. But we had set our goal, and we kept working away at it. We wanted to establish the habit of acknowledging God at the beginning of each new day and seeking His help.

Now, having said all this, the fact remains that, as parents, we can do little beyond trying to teach. By that I mean every child, as an individual, has to learn to know God and communicate with Him by himself. I cannot get into the heart of my child and on his behalf respond to God's love or bend his will to follow Him. My child has to do that on his own. My child has to learn to reach out for himself and appropriate the grace and help which he needs from God. In this realm, I, as a parent, stand helpless except for one thing. I can pray. And as I pray, God will work.

So don't get discouraged and don't give up. Be very sure we can leave no greater legacy with our children than teaching them to walk in harmony and communion with God and in teaching them to pray.

Family Religious Practices and Children

Two sociology professors at the University of Southern California, over a period of four years, conducted a survey among 2,044 members of a health-care plan used by a number of the Los Angeles-area labor unions. Nine hundred ninety-two people responded. Three generations were covered in the survey. The adults ranged in age from forty-five to sixty-four, the children from sixteen to twenty-six.

The survey showed that mothers have a far greater influence on children than fathers, with the exception of the area of religious behavior. If the father attends church regularly, the children will be more likely to attend regularly—regardless of the mother's attendance record. Few children attend if their parents do not. Parents who provide a less clear model (for example, the mother attends but the father doesn't) have children who vary widely in their churchgoing practices.

"This suggests two things," the study says. "First, parents who wish to transmit either a religious or nonreligious attitude can be more effective, if they clearly express this attitude themselves.

"Second, and perhaps more interesting, the parents can do even better if they practice their religious or nonreligious attitudes . . . thus [behavior] is not only most effective for transmitting religious behavior, but also for transmitting religious attitude."

The survey defined religious behavior as meaning membership and attendance and attitude as meaning depth of belief.

When a Mother Prays

Lord, help me to remember that nothing is going to happen to me today that You and I together can't handle.

Dear Lord, in this early-morning hour I am so glad to meet with You again. I want to kneel at Your feet and worship You.

(Sue's dress needs to be lengthened.)

How great You are! The birds are already singing outside, Father. Today will be another lovely day.

(Saturday is Dwight's birthday. Must send a card.)

Help me, Lord, to make this shining new day lovely in every way. Watch my lips. Guard my tongue. Hold my temper in check.

(I wonder if Dan got his confirmation work done. Must check and see.)

Watch over my husband as he drives the freeways.

(The payment on the insurance! It's due.)

Thank You for a wonderful husband, Father, and four healthy, strong children. Help each one. They are all so different. They need help in many ways, just as I do.

(Wonder how the Andrews baby is. Must call Betty.)

I need Your help, especially, Father, with that seventh-grade class I teach on Sundays.

(Jim has been absent three Sundays. Maybe a phone call to his mother will help.)

And then we have that big building program ahead of us at church. Show us what our share should be. Help us not to be

112

unduly anxious about the future. Help us to seek Your kingdom first.

(*Janet has a dental appointment this afternoon. Wonder how big our bill will be this time.*)

Bless our daughter who is away at college.

(*We haven't had a letter from her for three weeks—wonder why? Better call her tonight.*)

Keep her from serious illness. Help her with her problems. In her last letter, Lord, she wrote that she wished she was playing with dolls again instead of struggling to help humans with their problems. She's so young, Lord. Help her.

(*Is that toast I smell?*)

I think Dave is in the kitchen, Lord. I'll have to go. But, oh, I'm glad I'm your child and can live the whole day with You! Amen.

Does your praying or Bible reading ever get punctuated and interrupted like that?

For years I struggled with this problem. I sought to drive away distracting thoughts only to have them echo back again in a few minutes. Sometimes I would rise from my knees, and instead of feeling refreshed and strengthened I would be thoroughly upset, frustrated, and defeated.

Until at last I learned to do a very simple thing. Now when I kneel or sit to pray or read the Bible, I always put by my side a pad and a pencil. As the little reminder thoughts pop into my praying, I just catch them and jot them down. Treated in this way, they no longer boomerang back to me. And often at the end of a quiet time my day's schedule lies neatly written before me, too.

I don't think the Lord minds. He might even approve, for now I can come away from my quiet time relaxed, peaceful, and ready for that nice shining day stretching out ahead of me.

Parent's Prayer

O Heavenly Father, make me a better parent.

Teach me to understand my children, to listen patiently to what they have to say, and to answer all their questions kindly.

Keep me from interrupting them or contradicting them.

Make me as courteous to them as I would have them be to me.

Forbid that I should ever laugh at their mistakes, or resort to shame or ridicule when they displease me.

May I never punish them for my own selfish satisfaction or to show my power.

Let me not tempt my child to lie or steal.

And guide me hour by hour that I may demonstrate by all I say and do that honesty produces happiness.

Reduce, I pray, the meanness in me.

And when I am out of sorts, help me, O Lord, to hold my tongue.

May I ever be mindful that my children are children and I should not expect of them the judgement of adults.

Let me not rob them of the opportunity to wait on themselves and to make decisions.

Bless me with the bigness to grant them all their reasonable requests and the courage to deny them privileges I know will do them harm.

Make me fair and just and kind.

And fit me, O Lord, to be loved and respected and imitated by my children. Amen.

DR. GARRY C. MYERS

In the silences I make in the midst of the turmoil of life, I have appointments with God. From these silences, I come forth with spirit refreshed and with a renewed sense of power. I hear a Voice in the silences and become increasingly aware that it is the Voice of God. O how comforting is a little glimpse of God!

DAVID BRAINERD

O Lord, our God,
teach us
to ask for the right blessings.
Steer the vessel of our life towards Thyself,
　Thou tranquil haven of all storm-tossed souls.
Show us the course wherein we should go.
Renew a willing spirit within us.
Let Thy spirit curb our wayward desires
　and guide
　and enable us toward that which is our true good.
In all our work enable us to rejoice in Thy glorious and gladden-
　　ing presence.
For Thine is the glory and the praise forever and ever. Amen.

SAINT BASIL

The Business

I missed You
this morning,
Lord.
You were there.
　I wasn't.
I was too busy
　too soon.

IDA BARTON

How to Help the Bereaved Child

God calls our loved ones,
But we lose not wholly
What He hath given;
They live on earth
In thought and deed
As truly as in His heaven.
JOHN GREENLEAF WHITTIER

Brian was angry. It wasn't fair, he stormed. His dad had been getting well. The doctor had said he could come home from the hospital. And now he was dead. He'd never come home. There never would be any more fishing or camping trips.

Sheri, his fourteen-year-old sister, behaved differently. She cautiously locked the door of her self, pulled down the blinds, and stood looking at her mother as though through bars. And then she went to her room and shut the door.

What can you do to help a child who is experiencing bereavement and loss? I delved into books. I talked to friends: a Christian doctor, a pastor, two professors, a teacher in a parochial school, a nurse and mother who had been widowed twice, an African minister studying in the States, a professional counselor. For two days I sat with a group of fifteen mothers of varying ages. We talked and talked. This is what we decided:

The loss of a pet can introduce children to bereavement. The experience can be very painful. Not too long ago our children rescued a wounded bird. They transformed a shoe box into a hospital bed. Faithfully they masticated peanuts and bread to feed their invalid and carefully dropped water down its gaping beak.

One night our patient died. The next morning the shoe box became a coffin, a site was selected in the garden, a grave was dug.

116

I could not help noticing how the experience brought out the finest in the children. They forgot to disagree or quarrel but were tender and considerate.

Quickly replacing a pet that has died can rob the child of the refining benefits of grief. This loss can help prepare a child for greater bereavements to come.

When a child is faced with death, try to be understanding. For many children death is completely unreal. I was only eight when my sister died. I dearly loved her. Yet the day our phone rang with the news of Amy's sudden death, I went outside, jumped on the swing, and casually called out to my brother, "Amy's dead." The reality didn't strike me at all until the graveside service. Then suddenly I wanted to run away from it all.

So if a child seems casual and untouched by death, don't misinterpret it as "not caring." A child experiences life in an altogether different way from an adult. Don't make him feel guilty because he isn't feeling as bad as you think he should. Accept and love him as he is.

On the other hand, some children feel keenly and suffer greatly.

We were missionaries in East Africa when our five-year-old son lost his African playmate because of complications following measles. I found Dave lying on his bed, staring at the ceiling. Deeply hurt and puzzled, he had questions to ask. But after the questions, he resented any offers of sympathy and wanted only to be left alone.

David mourned the loss of his friend for weeks. Finally, after six months, when I thought he had recovered, we visited the village where Ephraim had been buried. I was startled when within minutes of our arriving there, Dave tugged at my sleeve and asked to be taken to Ephraim's grave. He stood by the rough, wooden cross and said sadly, "If you were here now, Ephraim, I'd let you ride my bike."

"I'll bet you would," I answered, "and the two of you would have lots of fun." Then I added, "Remember your favorite toy Land Rover you gave to Ephraim when he was sick?" Nod. "Did you know he was holding on tight to it when he died?"

Blurred eyes, tears, crying, and after that day it seemed the wound began to heal.

Let your child know you understand. Be sensitive to him. Respect his wishes. It can help to say things like: "I know you loved him very much," "You miss him, don't you?" "Dad would be real proud of you," "She loved you," "You always had fun playing together, didn't you?"

Try to maintain normalcy as much as possible. One mother related that when she was eleven, three close relatives died within a year's time. "A heavy spirit of gloom and sadness descended on our home," she recalled. "I thought I'd never know a happy time again. There were no birthday celebrations or parties or fun times all year."

Even more than adults, children seem to understand that life must go on. Ann McGrew wrote in *This Day* of her little girl whose pet dachshund was killed by a car. When her daddy carried in the limp body, Becky continued getting ready for school, wiping away tears as she searched for her books. Her mother asked her if she would like to stay home for the day. Becky's answer surprised her. She said simply, "I'm too sad to stay home."

Normalcy can be difficult, of course, if death has entered the home. But try to be hopeful.

One mother, who has been widowed twice, explained to her children that there would be tears, that sometimes she might cry a lot, but they should not worry. Tears, she told them, were good. She felt better after she had cried. And she assured them that though she was hurting very much now, it would get better, and they too wouldn't hurt so much after a while.

Some mothers felt extra effort should be made to provide outings or trips or visits with friends for the children to help them over the most difficult days.

Be truthful and direct. When Brian's and Sheri's father died, their mother called them to her room and quietly told them what had happened. She explained to them that now they would be only three, that some things wouldn't be easy, but that God would help.

The mothers in our group cautioned against using ambiguous terms or phrases which can conjure up frightening pictures such as : the Grim Reaper finally got old Joe; Ned bit the dust; Aunt Edna expired; or even, Grandma has fallen asleep forever. This last statement can produce a fear in children of falling asleep, lest for them too it be forever.

Answer their questions. The mother who at eleven had experienced multiple bereavements recalled: "I was worried and anxious and wanted, oh, so desperately to ask questions, but I didn't dare. I felt the grown-ups already had more problems than they could cope with without my asking difficult questions."

All the mothers underscored the need for a listening ear. Some felt children should be encouraged to ask questions.

Be sure you don't load your child with responsibilities that were never meant for young shoulders. In other words, don't say, "You'll have to be Mother (or Father) from now on."

Be alert to fears that might develop out of the experience. A couple of weeks after Ephraim's death, Dave was stricken. As he lay burning with fever, he pleaded with me to sleep with him at night and wanted me with him at all hours. I could understand why and complied willingly, trying to reassure him that the doctor was caring for him and he soon would be well.

One of the mothers of our group said that she was eight when her mother died, and she lived in great fear that her father would die too. She recalled gratefully that her father took time out to talk to her often, to explain things, and to reassure her.

One mother said they had reached an agreement with another couple that if death came to both parents this couple would care for their children. The children knew about this, and it seemed to bring them comfort and security.

What about funerals? Most mothers felt that it was a good thing to allow children to attend funerals. Otherwise they often let their imagination run wild. They suggested preparing the child for it, however, explaining just what the child would see and what would be done.

One mother cautioned that they be sure the funeral would be conducted in a quiet manner. As a child she had attended funerals where there was unrestrained weeping and wailing. It had scarred her so badly that only in the last couple of years, as her own faith in God had grown, had she been able to even think of going to a funeral.

Emphasize the good points and qualities in the life of the one who has died. Recall fun times. Show slides or movies from the times when they were together. Tell of the big dreams and hopes the parent or grandparent had for the children. Get them to aspire to the highest. Recall times when the parent or grandparent derived much joy from the children. Leave with them the assurance that they were dearly loved.

Accept the help and comfort the children can give you. A father wrote: "I remember when our first boy passed away, and we were traveling homeward in a great deal of sorrow. Peter, then six years of age, said that Terry was now in heaven and happy, and that we ought to be happy too. This changed the attitude of all of us at that particular time."

The parents' attitude will do the most for the child during this time. We cannot escape the sorrow and tears that come with death, but if, through the tears, the child can witness times of joy and peace, it will help. "I go,"Adoniram Judson declared as he lay dying, "with the gladness of a boy bounding away from school. I feel so strong in God." If parents can let their children know that they face death in this spirit, they will be helping in the greatest way possible.

When Grandma Visits Us

". . . Night is drawing nigh—"
For all that has been—Thanks!
For all that shall be—Yes!

DAG HAMMARSKJÖLD

Dear Mother:

Thank you for coming to visit us. Our family needs your visits.

We need to be reminded that people grow old. There are so few older people on our block, and those there are we never talk to. There's a sprinkling of older folks at church, but there we're all divided into little age groups. Except on Sundays, when we all smile at each other and say we're fine, even if we're not.

Of course, you say that all the time. After you'd been here, eleven-year-old David said: "Ever notice how Grandma always says, 'Well, it sure isn't worth complaining about!'?"

I still tell my friends about your indignant remark one day when I asked you how you were. You brushed back a stray gray lock and said impatiently, fire in your faded eyes, "If you didn't ask so many questions, I wouldn't have to tell so many lies!"

We know you've lied to us. Like the day we'd planned to go to Disneyland, and your knees were big with arthritis. With difficulty you got in and out of boats and trains that day, but you weren't going to miss a single ride. You just hung on tight and screamed with all the kids and laughed when we got stuck down in the caverns of the Pirates of the Caribbeans.

You're tough. Tough with the toughness of a widow. The toughness of an immigrant's child. The toughness of a child of the soil.

121

Our seventeen-year-old, six-foot-two son, grubbing out a tree trunk from our yard, paused to wipe the sweat off his forehead and exclaim, "How'd Grandma ever grub out that stump from her lawn?" How did you? How did you ever climb up and nail shingles back on the roof when the storm ripped them off? You're embarrassed now when I mention it. You stare at the floor. "Shucks," you say, "that's nothing."

We've gone soft. We need your toughness. We don't want to hobble through life leaning on chemical crutches. You demo strate a better way.

We need your perspective on life too.

How much has happened in the course of your life. You remember all the stages: walking, horse and buggy, train, car, airplane (and how you love to fly!).

You began life when nature was a cruel enemy which threatened to kill you—by too much rain or not enough, by storms and cyclones and freezing winter.

Wrestling with Mother Earth and the forces of nature in order to eke out the necessities of life demanded all your time and lots of hard work. Now when things are easier, you are appalled by the mustard pall hovering overhead, threating to drop down and choke us. You fought for survival. We fight for survival. It's just on a different basis.

Your faith that God will take care of us is unshakable. Doesn't He hold history in His hand? you ask. Didn't He care for you all your life? Over and over you recount the tales I know so well I could repeat them backwards. Sometimes I've chafed inwardly at the repetition. But unconsciously you have taught well. I remember what you have said.

Sometimes you become overwhelmed, as we all do. You sit and listen quietly as we talk about today's problems and how they can be solved. And then you get up and walk slowly to your room, and I notice that your shoulders droop as though all your seventy-eight years have suddenly descended on you, and your walk is tired.

But a night's rest—even if you sleep little these days—restores you.

"I wash and flatten my cans for recycling," you say as you

help me prepare dinner. Unconsciously, you are more ecology minded than I am. You like my garbage-disposal unit, but patiently you continue to dig your garbage into the ground. You scorn throwaways. The first thing you did when you moved to your new place was plant fruit trees. "For those who follow me," you said.

You are more frugal in your use of water and electricity than I am. Your clothes blow dry in the sun and wind. "They smell good," you say. You scoop up the lint from my lint trap in the dryer. "What happens to clothes when all this comes off?" you ask.

You prize the possessions you have had for many years and are proud that they have lasted so long. That silver hand mirror you have had for fifty-seven years. When the handle broke you had it welded on. New things hold little interest for you. "Don't buy me anything more," you plead. "The house is full."

But shrubs and flowers for your garden are welcome. An airline ticket that will enable you to strengthen family relationships you cherish. A railing you can hang on to when you come down your narrow, steep stairs. And you love a trip to new places to see new things and learn.

When you talk of death, you make us feel homeless in this world, and this is good.

"Grandma talks so much of dying, She must think of it every day," one of our daughters observed.

"Probably. She's getting ready for a journey, and talking about it helps her get ready," I explained.

The children fell silent. They were thinking. They need to think about these things—we all do. Otherwise how will we be prepared for it when it happens in our family?

So, thank you, Mother, for coming to visit us. Your plane is winging you back home as I write this. In your little notebook you are making notes in your even, rounded handwriting: How high you are flying, the speed, the temperature outside. You will ask the stewardess if they really do throw away the plastic dishes you eat from. Secretly within your heart maybe you are hoping your plane will be hijacked to Cuba. Wouldn't that be an experience?

You are preparing for a transition to a better life—impatiently accepting it and adjusting to the restrictions of your age (though cheating a little on your diet once in a while)—thinking every day about death and at the same time busy learning all you can about life.

God bless you, Mother dear. Come again. We need you now more than ever.

We thank you, our Father,
that you have been with us this day.
In a few hours we shall go to bed.
Go with each of us to rest.
If any awake,
    make the dark hours of watching endurable.
When day returns,
    return to us,
    Our Sun and Comforter.
Call us up
    with morning faces
    and morning hearts
eager to work,
    eager to be happy, if happiness should be our portion.
And if the day be marked for sorrow,
    make us strong to endure it. Amen.

ROBERT LOUIS STEVENSON

O Lord Jesus Christ,
Thou Good Shepherd of the sheep,
who camest to seek the lost and to gather them into Thy fold,
    have compassion upon those who have wandered from Thee;

feed those who hunger,
cause the weary to lie down in Thy pastures,
bind up those who are broken in heart,
and strengthen those who are weak,
that we, relying on Thy care and being comforted by Thy love,
may abide in Thy guidance to our lives' end.

ANCIENT COLLECT

We beseech Thee that this day
   Thy strength would pilot us,
   Thy power preserve us,
   Thy wisdom instruct us,
   Thy eye watch over us,
   Thy ear hear us,
   Thy Word give us sweet talk,
   Thy hand defend us, and
   Thy way guide us.

SAINT PATRICK